Napoleon is one of the most illuminating figures in modern history. He was a man of extraordinary qualities and at the same time suffered from extraordinary failings. His ambition was power, his dream, a vast empire, and his passion, wars and victories. People loved him and presented him with power, gave him their sons to satisfy his passion for continuous warfare till he exhausted France of her manpower. Great kingdoms collapsed before him and all Europe trembled at his name. He terrorised many kings into subjugation till he was subjugated himself in a fateful battle and met his end in a tragic manner as the 'Prisoner of Europe'.

Here is the story of this dauntless man, the story of the great French Revolution from which this brilliant commander emerged; the story of his striking military campaigns, his mighty wars and conquests, his colourful love-affairs and the women who ruled him; and the story of intrigues that surrounded him and led to his downfall.

Emil Ludwig's 'Napoleon' is a great book of modern times. His masterly handling of a historical subject and his superb presentation of the life of an outstanding man and a thrilling chapter of history, make this book a classic.

In May, the Corsicans were defeated. There was a terrible retreat through the dense forests and the rugged mountains. Among the multitude of men and the few women, rode Letizia, big with child, carrying her one-year-old boy in her arms, seated on a mule. They reached the coast safely. In June the defeated Paoli, accompanied by a few hundred of his faithful followers, had to flee to Italy. In July Paoli's adjutant, Letizia's husband, with other envoys, capitulated to the conqueror. The insular pride was humbled. But in August his wife brought the avenger into the world.

She named him Napolione.

This woman, who during the campaign had played the heroine and had shown a man's courage, must now, in the great house by the sea-shore, become a prudent and thrifty housewife, Her young husband, fanciful by temperament, lived more on plans than on income. For years his energies were mainly devoted to the great lawsuit concerning his inheritance. As a student in Pisa, where among his fellows he was known as Count Buonaparte, he had lived well but learned little. After the birth of his second son, he cut his studies short. How was he to make a living? In troublous times, a man of the world takes the world as it is; comes to terms with the conqueror; all the more since the French in order to secure their footing in the island, are inclined to show favour to the Corsican nobility.

Soon he becomes assessor in the new lawcourts; superintendent of a nursery in which the King of France, eager to turn the new possessions to account, wishes to grow mulberries; and when the distinguished marshal comes to stay, no expense must be spared. There are still flocks of sheep in the hills and vineyards along the coast; his brother, archdeacon at the cathedral, is well-to-do; and his wife's half brother, another priest, a merchant's son, is skilled in worldly affairs.

By the time his proud and beautiful wife has reached her thirties, five boys and three girls have been born to her. This is well accordant to the notions of the islanders, for whom rivalries and vendettas are supreme virtues. But the rearing of eight children is a costly matter; so, day by day, the youngsters hear their parents talking about money. At length, however, the father finds a way out of his difficulties. Accompanied by his two eldest sons, now ten and eleven years of age, he sails to France, and journeys from Toulon to Versailles.

He brings recommendations from the marshal in Corsica. The Buonapartes' Italian title of nobility is confirmed by the Herald's College in Paris. To the Corsican official who has been loyal for a decade, King Louis makes a grant of two thousand francs. The two sons and one of the daughters are given scholarships in the Nobles' Schools: One son is to be a priest; the other, an officer.

III

A taciturn boy, small, shy, and lonely, sits reading in a corner of the garden. It is his own plot in the school garden at Brienne, and he has made a fence round it. Really, only a third of the enclosure is his own, for he has fenced in the plots of neighbours on either side. They may come in too; but woe to any one else who disturbs his privacy! He rushes furiously at the intruder. A little while ago, when the boys had a fireworks' display, two of his schoolmates, who had been slightly burned, had run away to his garden for refuge. He had driven them out, flourishing a hoe at them.

No punishment will bring him to reason in this matter. The masters shake their heads and let him go his own way.

"The youngster is made of granite," says one of them, "but there is a volcano inside."

No one may touch this little kingdom of his in the garden, though part of it is usurped. He has an ardent feeling for his own independence. Writing to his father, he says: "I would rather be the first among the workmen in a factory than the last among the artists in the Academy." Did he get the idea out of Plutarch? Certainly he has an enthusiasm for that author, the lives of the

This was too much for the Lyons Academy, which declared the essay "unworthy of commendation." A fresh disappointment! The effort had brought neither money nor renown. With indefatigable assiduity, none the less, he resumes work on his Corsican novel, and pens a dialogue on love.

What? Does this word, too, shed its lustre into the youth's sombre mind? Are we to have an outpouring in the Rousseauist vein? Hearken to the words of our Lieutenant, now twenty two years of age: "I, too, was in love once, and learned enough of it to despise definition, which only confuse the issue. I deny its justification; nay, more, I regard it as injurious to society and destructive to the happiness of the individual. Men could bless heaven if they were quit of it."

Fanfares interrupt these political and social muslins, fanfares from Paris! Louis XVI, attempting to escape, had been caught at Varennes and brought back. The people had triumphed, and the revolutionary movement was intensified. On the second anniversary of the taking of the Bastille, the Red Lieutenant proposed a toast to the patriots. From the island came to him sounds of confusion, the heartbeats of anarchy—for during these wild years the ripples of turbulence spread from Paris in widening circles, to reach distant shores. In Corsica, too, civil war is imminent. Back there, for a second venture!

VIII

Now the lieutenant has to play the part of Coriolanus. Catch voices, catch men; for, since the people have come into power, it is necessary to cultivate popularity. Archdeacon Lucien Buonaparte has chosen this convenient hour for dying, and the family is in easier circumstances. Mother's brother Fesch, another cleric, has been prevailed upon to join the Jacobin Club. Joseph can influence opinion in the town council. Is there any other man in the island competent to direct a battery? Of course the leader of the National Guard would have the real power in his hand. But suppose one should fail to secure election?

This time his furlough lasts only till the new year. Better be careful! He writes to his commanding officer: "Urgent circumstances have forced me to outstay my leave. But I have nothing to reproach myself with: more sacred duties, tenderer obligations, are my excuse." He hopes that he will not be cashiered. No answer! Well, he must take the risk.

Now comes the election of the commandant of the National Guard. Kinsmen everywhere, but that does not suffice. His mother keeps open house for party friends; often sympathisers from the hills have to be put up for the night; this is the way to catch votes. "At that time," writes a comrade, "he would for a season be taciturn and reflective; then he would be genial once more, pleasant to all comers, conversationally inclined, prepared to visit any one who might be of use, and doing his utmost to win adherents." When the commissaries come, he has one of them forcibly detained in his house; and he arranges that the supporters of a rival shall have a thrashing. This is a Corsican election! But when the palpitating day draws to a close, Napoleon has gained his end. He is second in command, with the rank of lieutenant colonel.

Shall he seize the opportunity, this Italian, of sending in his papers in France? Shall he leave the French service? Better be careful, still! From the memoirs of great commanders he has learned that it is always wise to leave a line of retreat open. "In this difficult posture of affairs," he writes to Valence, "a good Corsican's post of honour is in his native country. That is why my own folk keep me from returning to France. Since, however, I am not one to compromise where duty is concerned, I had it in mind to resign my commission." But, far from sending in his papers, he asks for arrears of pay, and actually speaks of France as "your nation." In answer, he is cashiered by the French military authorities.

Thus he has become a soldier of fortune more speedily than he had wished. He is without firm standing-ground; his only rights are the revolutionary rights of a National Guardsman, the member of a force which may go to pieces directly a reverse is sustained. Hic Rhodus! He must take advantages of the latent civil war

own age occupy prominent positions. Only he, with his surging thoughts and imaginative schemes, remains lonely and does nothing.

"If you are going away for a long time," he writes to Joseph, "send me your portrait. We have lived so long in close companionship that our hearts are intertwined. No one knows better than you how wholly I am yours. As I write these lines, I am more moved than almost ever before, feeling that it will be long before we meet again. I cannot write any more, Frarewell, mon ami."

He is in a melting mood, and at times he seems utterly discouraged. "To clamber upwards from step to step, this is rather like an adventurer, like a man who is trying to make happiness." Finally he says: "Life is a trivial dream, which fades away....."

XIII

Suddenly everything is in flux. A new Minister for War has been appointed, and he is eager to effect changes on the Italian front. Does any one know of a new man to whom the command there can be entrusted? The enquiry passes from one to another, until someone recommends Buonaparte. He is summoned to the War Office. For years he has been making himself familiar with the Italian coast and the Italian frontier, and forthwith he expounds a detailed plan for a campaign in northern Italy, against Sardinia and Austria. It is substantiated by a display of intimate knowledge of the Alpine passes; of the weather and the snows of seed-time and harvest; of the administration, the temperament, and the characteristics of the territories and the populations concerned. After the conquest of Lombardy, between February and July, the powerful position of Mantua must be wrested from the Austrians. Then the Army of Italy must move northward, and in Tyrol must effect a junction with the sister army, the Army of the Rhine. The joint forces will threaten Vienna and this will compel the emperor to accept a peace which will fulfil all that France has been expecting or imagining for years past.

Overwhelmed by the cataract that issues from this brain, the minister can only say: "Your ideas, General, are equally brilliant and bold. We must examine them closely. Write a report for the committee. You can take your time."

"My plan is ready now. I can write it down in half an hour."

"A notable design," say the members of the Committee of Public Safety when the report has been read to them; "notable, even if impracticable." In any case, such an intelligence as this must be utilised in the Operations Department. A few days afterwards he has a seat in this department, where everything is decided.

The great moment has come, the turning point of his youth. At length he stands on the threshold of his career. The chance has come suddenly, for everything is sudden in this eruptive era. From now, when he is barely twenty-six, he will for twenty years, with unremitting vigour, move onwards towards his goal, drawing the chain of thought and action after him. Suddenly, twenty years hence, the chain will snap.

Napoleon's work begins. With burning energy, attending carefully to little things because his aim is the greatest of things, he devotes himself to "affairs." The veil is lifted, for here he finds the most secret reports concerning all the armies of the republic. At the same time, his daily association with the leading civilian figures in France gives him authority. The suggestive influence of his personality makes itself felt.

What is the first thing he aspires to gain for himself? Neither the command in Vendée nor the command of the Army of the Rhine. These are attainable, tangible magnitudes. Here, at the centre of all the real fronts, nothing allures him so much as the thought of a command which as yet lives only in his imagination; in a battle ground which does not exist, but which he wants to create today, and which he will again want to create seventeen years hence. Asia! Directly he gets to work at the centre of things, he begins to emphasise the importance of galvanising Turkey into activity, of introducing artillery and the modern art of war on the Bosphorus, for in due time they can from that centre be used

epistolary campaign, carried on side by side with a campaign of cavalry and by guns, waged with the same ardour and the same success. "You are asking me to perform miracles, and I cannot do that.... Only with prudence and foresight can we achieve great ends. It is but a step from victory to defeat. In affairs of magnitude I have learned that, in the last resort, everything invariably turns upon the trifle." But to Carnot, the great army organiser, to whom he can say much that is unsuitable for his official dispatches, he writes, gnashing his teeth: "Would you believe it, that I have not a single engineer officer here, not one who has ever taken part in a siege! You can hardly conceive how furious I am that I have no artillery!" His actual resources totalled 24 mountain guns, 4,000 underfed horses, frs. 300,000 in silver, and enough food to supply his 30,000 men for a month on half rations. With these vestiges of an equipment, he is to conquer Italy!

Nevertheless, having undertaken the venture, he makes the best of the materials at his disposal. Getting to work like a hurricane upon this crowd of pitiful men who have run to seed, upon crops some of which have already begun to sing the royal anthem again, with indefatigable energy he succeeds in transforming them into a republican army.

Here are some of his doings on the third day after his arrival. Sending a hundred and ten workmen to make a road. Suppression of a mutiny in a brigade. Quartering of two artillery divisions. Orders to two generals in case of horse stealing. Answer to the requests of two others concerning their commands. Order to a general in Toulon to bring his men to Nice. Order to another general to find the most efficient officer in the mutinous brigade. Address to the general staff. Review of troops with orders of the day. –During the first twenty days, one hundred and twenty-three written orders relate solely to the provisioning of the troops; among them are numerous complaints concerning peculation, short weight and inferior goods; and these orders are issued on the march, from twelve different headquarters, in the interludes between six skirmishes.

For hardly has he passed through the narrow defiles than, in accordance with this new principle, he has massed his forces to attack first one and then the other of the allied foes, and in two battles he defeats and separates them. In truth, these were mere advance-guard skirmishes, as becomes the nature of the French, and the previous training of these troops, which as yet know nothing of the great movement in open lines. At this stage of his campaign, speed and boldness are more important than elaborate strategy.

When he is on one of these breathless rides, in the deep mountain valleys, through the passes, amid the thunder of his own and the enemy cannon, suddenly the glass covering Josephine's miniature (with he carries in the inner pocket of his tunic, and has kissed hundreds of times) shivers into fragments. Growing paler than ever, he reins in his charger, and says to Bourrienne: "The glass is broken. My wife is ill or unfaithful. Forward!"

Everything depends upon the fulfilment of his first old pledge. He knows that if, this once, he is able to do what he has promised, the army will believe him; and if it believes him, it will soon believe in him. In actual fact, a fortnight after his prophecy had been uttered, the army, which had won its first victories on entering the downward grade, found itself on the last elevation. The soldiers raised a hearty cheer. After the weary days in the narrow valleys, they at length caught sight of the plains of Piedmont lying at their feet, stretching out into the immeasurable distance, blossoming in the spring weather, offering all that they had gone short of for so long. The Po and other rivers were flowing towards the horizon, and at length the world of snows lay behind. "As if by a magician's spell, they had been enabled to cross the gigantic barrier, which had seemed to them like the frontier of another world."

"All this is yours!" Their commander has forced one of the two opponents, the King of Sardinia, to make truce, thus compelling the surrender of everything that grows on Sardinian territory. This first truce of his campaigns was secured by Bonaparte through cunning and bluff, for he threatened the enemy with the

degrees.... Be less beautiful, less tender, and above all less jealous. Your tears inflame my blood.... Join me quickly, so that, before we die, we may be able to say: 'We have had so many happy days!' A million kisses, even for your horrid Fortune!"

Neither now nor later could the commander-in-chief rid his home of this lap-dog. He tells us that on his wedding night the dog was in bed with Josephine. "I had to choose between sleeping beside the beast or not sleeping with my wife. A terrible dilemma, but I had to take it or leave it. I resigned myself. The dog was less accommodating. I have the marks on my leg to show what he thought about the matter!"

Amid the hurly-burly, the general's lady arrives at Brescia. Almost immediately she has to be sent back to Milan. She has a narrow escape of being seized by the enemy, together with some recruits and cannon. Now she has an excuse, and, in the future, she will be slower to comply with his invitations.

During these weeks, Bonaparte for the first time loses courage, though it is only for a few hours of one night. Instead of simply issuing orders. He holds a council of war, much to the astonishment of his generals. In this critical situation, he proposes to retreat across the Po, but the mad Augereau thumps the table, shouting: "For the sake of your own fame, I insist that we attack." He flings from the room. The counsels of the others are divided.

See him before the decision, brooding over his maps. He is alone. Moths are fluttering round the candles, and at last burn themselves to death. The midsummer night is sultry. As he listens to the drums and the shouting without, he thinks: "Tomorrow will settle whether we can keep Lombardy. Perhaps it will be the turning point in my destiny. Shall I stake all on one card? What if Wurmser's strength is greater than the reports say? Josephine is sleeping now, in the great bed. Or, who knows, she may be laughing softly in the embrace of some puppy who has bewitched her.

He decides to fight. Next day, he is victorious at Castiglione.

Soon afterwards, he writes: "Three days without a letter from you; I have written daily. This separation is terrible; the nights are long and savourless, the days monotonous.: At this time, Josephine writes to Tallien in Paris: "I am bored to death." He is busied in battles and victories; she is fêted and honoured. To both of them life seems wearisome: to him, because she is too far away; to her, because he is too near. Three days later: "The enemy has been beaten, my darling. Eighteen thousand prisoners, the others dead or wounded. Wurmser has only Mantua left. This is the biggest success yet; Italy, Friuli, and Tyrol are saved for the republic. In a few days we shall see one another again, that is the reward for labour and pains. A thousand glowing kisses!"

When the commander can draw breath, the statesman must turn every moment to account. In Modena he assembles deputies from all the States as far south as Bologna, and at a formal sitting he gives them a constitution, that they may unite to form henceforward one State, the new republic. Is he happy, now that he is at work State-building? His wife in Milan must be in love with someone, or she would write to him differently.

"Your letters are cold" —this is from Modena on the same day. "Their tone suggests that we must have been married for half a century at least. Friendship and winter, it is odious and spiteful. What more am I to expect of you? That you have ceased to love me? That is an old story. That you should hate me? Well and good. That is what I wish. Everything degrades, save only hatred. But indifference with a heart of marble, lack lustre eyes, languid gait?... A thousand kisses, tender as my heart."

Fresh crises call him northward once more, He comes, he fights, he is driven back. The gloomy November weeks, in which his fate again trembles in the balance, are not gladdened by any consolation from her. Far from it, for his most intimate friends, alive to all that goes on in Milan, venture cautious hints that my lady Josephine is having a merry time. This is the day after the defeat at Caldiero. He sends to Paris a despairing appeal for reinforcements.

Complications thicken; courage wanes; everyone turns for help to the chief. He seems to be thinking with thirty heads these days when the battle of Arcola is impending, It is in a crazy mood

VIII

A high-arched room, in the baroque style; the walls are white, picked out with gold. On a long couch upholstered in green silk, a sixteen year old lieutenant, a spoiled darling, with the fawning manners of a page, is sitting between two women of ripe beauty. One of them is the youth's mother; but when her smiling glance roves coquettishly over the surrounding group of smartly dressed officers, we gather that she is thinking far less of maternal obligations than of hours in which such boys as hers are engendered. Without words, she seems to add: "Creole women are adepts in the art of love!" Another connoisseur in the same art is the handsome general who stands behind her, craning forward over her shoulder that he may see far down into her corsage—as fashion and the lady's pride in her charms make it easy for him to do. This is Masséna, whose talent as a soldier is to be ever prompt to attack, being too unrestrained and uncultured to count the cost; but his flaming impetuosity often saves his troops in moments of danger. His temperament is so ardent, that he must always have at least two women in his train; and his appetite for money is no less keen. Money and women—he steals both, whenever he has the chance.

All the qualities that Masséna lacks, you will find in the little man with the big head who stands in front of the ladies making conversation. He is ugly, touchingly grotesque in his movements, and at the moment intoxicated by his success in winning—no one knows how—the love of a pretty member of the Visconti family. This is Berthier, chief of general staff, unresting in his activity; a man who will do administrative work one day, and take a fortress by storm the next; a great student of maps, for he is one of the few among these officers who is well grounded in the theory of his profession.

There is Murat, theatrically decked out in green satin, twisting the huge plumed hat he holds in his hands. Of proletarian birth, like most of the men at this remarkable headquarters, he is fond of talking in asides. Now he laughs too loudly because the ribald Augereau, the avaricious and extravagant peasant's son, has been telling him an after-dinner story. Murat, though he fears neither artillery fire nor the frowns of princes, is now painfully embarrassed because Josephine calls to him across the room. She wants to hear the joke!

But Joseph, a man of the world, who dreads what the enfant terrible may blurt out, nods meaningly to Murat, implying to him that for God's sake he must hold his tongue. Elise is sitting in the embrasure of one of the windows. Not so good-looking as the other women, and finding her husband a bore, she is apt to be censorious, and would carry tales to Mother Letizia, who abhors Josephine's loose morals.

Now comes the bright sound of laughter from the garden. That is Pauline's birdlike voice. She is making the most of the days of freedom left to her before her marriage to General Leclerc, the husband chosen for her by Napoleon. She is playing blindman's-bluff with Hippolyte, and her pleasure in the game is doubled by the knowledge that she is annoying Josephine.

Here is the chief, coming slowly along the passage. For two long hours he has been walking up and down with the Parisian dramatist Arnault. This compartion has been carefully chosen. The newcomer has asked many questions about the army and the battles. Bonaparte has answered them with a detailed report of his own doings, which he knows that Arnault will spread far and wide. Now he has steered the conversation to the topic of the governmental crisis, long drawn out. As the two come into the reception room, he says, ostensibly with indifference, and yet with emphasis enough to fix the words in Arnault's memory: "I can hardly conceive any other way out of their difficulties than that they should bend before the power of one strong man. But where is such a man to be found?"

As Bonaparte enters, the officers rise to their feet, break off all conversation, and look expectantly at this man of twenty-seven, though most of them are older than he and all of them a good deal

Applause, as usual; but is there one among these thousands, even among those in the inner councils, who realises the profound truth of the closing phrase? Does any one of the auditors feel the poignancy of the satire?

Napoleon quietly comes to the front. What is he going to say?

"The French nation had to fight with its kings in order to win freedom.... Religion, feudalism, monarchy, have in turn ruled Europe for two thousand years. The era of democratic constitutions has only just begun. It has been your achievement to extend the domain of the Great Nation to its natural frontiers. You have done more. The two loveliest countries of Europe, renowned for science, art, and genius, see the spirit of freedom, buoyed up by hope, rising out of the tombs of their ancestors. These are the pedestals on which two mighty nations are uplifted. I have the honour to present you the treaty of Campo Formio, ratified by Emperor Francis.... As soon as the fortunes of the French nation are established upon the best organic laws, Europe, too, will be free."

The soldierly voice is silent. For a moment, not a sound is to be heard. Then come salvos of applause. Are they applauding the speech? It lacks the charm of the popular orations and the speeches from the tribune with which the walls of Paris are often placarded. The hearers are astonished; many of them are positively amazed. Alarm and veneration are the prevailing sentiments. The applause is not for the speech, but for the man. He has spoken on many fronts, has harangued a crowd in Corsica, but has never before addressed society folk, or politicians.

His speech was that of a statesman. At first perhaps not a soul but Talleyrand understood it. All that he had said of their own epoch, seemed false. England and America had been democracies for many, many years. France had been fighting nearly a decade for her recognition as a democracy. Now, at last, recognition had come, in this peace with Germany. There was the tangible proof of it in the parchment which betokened peace on the Continent.

them savage by disposition, but the dread with which this man fills me is a thing apart. He is neither good nor bad, neither gentle nor cruel. He is unique; he can neither inspire nor feel affection; he is more and less than a man. Character, mind, speech – all have a strange stamp. This very strangeness helps him to win over the French.

"He neither hates nor loves; for him, no one exists but himself; all other people are merely 'number so-and-so.' A great chessplayer, for whom humanity at large is the adversary he hopes to checkmate. His success is quite as much due to the qualities he lacks as to the qualities he possesses.... Where his own interest is involved, he pursues it as the just man seeks virtue; if his aim were good, his perseverance would be exemplary.... He despises the nation whose applause he seeks; there is not a spark of fervour intermingled with his craving to astound mankind.... I have never been able to breathe freely in his presence."

If we discount in these sentences all that may reasonably be regarded as due to the mortified vanity of a notable and much admired woman, enough will still remain to be worthy of careful study. Each moment she tries to pierce his armour, only in the next breath to acknowledge herself his prisoner. She moves in Rousseauist world of abstract virtue and goodness, with which a dictator can have nothing to do, and she therefore cannot regard Bonaparte with enthusiasm; but nevertheless she foresees his aim, which was not publicity disclosed till near the end of his career, and hers is the credit of having been the first to recognise his genius.

"Picture to yourself a little man," writes a German at this date in one of his letters home. "No taller than Frederick the Great; very regularly and slenderly built; lean, but sturdy; a large head; high forehead; dark-grey eyes; thick, dark-brown hair; Grecian nose, so long that it almost hangs down over the mouth; his mouth is full of humaneness and grace; the firm chin is rather prominent. His movements are brisk, but he has a fine and dignified bearing. You may see him run down a long staircase in five or six strides, and yet, as he finished the last stride, he stands before you as

doned. Sometimes he goes for a ride, in spite of the heat. When, on his return, he finds that no dispatches have come, he grows meditative:

"Do you know what I have been thinking. Bourrienne?-If I ever see France again, my greatest ambition will be to conduct a campaign on the Bavarian lowland. There I could win a great battle, and take vengeance for Blenheim. Then I should retire to my country seat, and lead a quiet life, perfectly contented." The fire still glows; the kettle goes on simmering! In the plain of the Po, his restless spirit was yearning for the East; having made his way to Egypt, he craves for Bavaria; and always thinks in terms of battles.

Now, when his future is so uncertain, when he is perhaps cut off from all chance of returning home, and when there is no longer a strong tie of personal affection to bind him to distant Europe, he opens negotiations with the Shah of Persia and Tippoo Sahib, England's enemies: asking the former for a right of way to India; and offering the latter an alliance, and deliverance from "The iron yoke of England." The prospect of following in Alexander's footsteps looms nearer. But when he comes to practical calculations he begins to doubt the possibility: "Only if fifteen thousand men can be left here, and I have another thirty thousand at my disposal, shall I be able to venture a march on India."

Although all remains in the realm of fancy, such imaginative excursions fill Bonaparte's happiest hours; he luxuriates in these vast plans. Four years later, he declares: "in Egypt alone did I feel free from the trammels of civilisation; and there I seemed to have the means of realising all my dreams. I pictured myself on the road to Asia, the founder of a new religion, mounted on an elephant, wearing a turban, and holding a new Koran which contained my own message. My plan was to weld the experiences of two worlds, to force history into my service, to attack the English power in India, and, through my conquests there, to reopen communications with Europe."

Are these the visions of a poet? Or is it that the conqueror and the poet are close kin? In Egypt, he has a romantic name for himself, "Sultan El Kebir" -he is, in truth, always the sultan, more or less. El Kebir is his third name, as visionary as the whole campaign.

His lively imagination, his spleen on account of his wife's infidelity-those combine with the influences of climate and lack of occupation to drive him into an amourette. A pretty young woman, the wife of a lieutenant, had sailed with the army from Toulon, in male attire. She was the illegitimate daughter of a cook, had herself been a dressmaker before marriage, was piquant, blonde, violet-eyed. He takes her to himself, and sends her husband back to France on official service. She soons learn to play Cleopatra's part boldly and charmingly; grace the head of his table; drives out with him. But Eugene, her rival's son, is adjutant, and his duty is to follow the carriage on horseback. This conjuncture is disagreeable to all parties, and so the young man is given furlough.

Eugene knows more than he cares to know about the scandal attaching to his mother's name; Bonaparte has himself enlightened the youth. What a painful situation! His mother, not far on in the thirties, is a coquette, and, makes his stepfather (the hero of the nation!) ridiculous in all men's eyes by her open and shameless intrigue with a young coxcomb who is but little older than her son. Eugene himself has to look on while Napoleon, commander-in-chief of the army and pasha of a new French colony, flaunts his mistress before the public gaze. The little dressmaker, who would probably find the handsome adjutant more to her taste than his stepfather, laughs gaily, showing her white teeth. Anyhow, she has cut out the Creole countess, and she glories in the new spirit of equality. Napoleon Bonaparte is the central figure of the composition. All he asks of the young woman is that she shall give him a child.

An heir, that is what he has been wanting for years! If she will but provide one, he will marry her, for divorces can be arranged. One of his ruling passions is the desire to found a family. The mother would be of working class origin? So are most of his generals! What matter, so long as the child is legitimate, and of the blood of Bonaparte? He believes in the equality of all who

charms, or she would not have so many admirers. What a fool, compared with her, was that little woman in Egypt, and even she could not give me an heir. Where shall I find a woman who will make a more perfect lover and a better wife than Josephine? Besides, she has had two children, and may yet have more."

He opens the door and, heroic in his silence, suppresses, once and for all, the accusations with which his heart is filled, in this matter, as in others, he holds fast to his resolves. Next day she confesses that she is in debt to the tune of two million francs. He pays without a word.

It is hard for his brother, and still harder for his sisters, to accept the situation; but they do not venture a remonstrance.

Nor is there time for the further discussion of family matters. Events are on the wing. His brothers have not been idle while he has been away. Joseph, after being envoy in Rome, is now on guard as one of the Parisian deputies. Lucien is leader of the opposition, although, being only twenty-four, he is under the legal age. A brilliant orator, dreaded in debate, a Hotspur with a taste for theatrical displays, burning with ambition, too headstrong for constructive work. He and Sieyés have been working at plans for a coup d'état on their own, but they lack the support of a great soldier whom the troops would follow. Now the soldier has come, and Lucien will keep his private wishes to himself. He, too, is a Bonaparte.

Dangerous, inscrutable, and cunning is Joseph's new brother-in-law, Bernadotte. He is slow in coming to greet Bonaparte. When he does come, and Bonaparte speaks of the desperate situation of the republic. Bernadotte rejoins: "It will be able to make headway against its enemies both abroad and at home!" He looked searchingly at his interlocutor, and for a moment the masterful eyes of the two men clash. But Bonaparte, controlling his emotions as usual, attempts a diversion to political issues, speaks again of the dangers, and then passes severe strictures on the Jacobin Club. Thereupon Bernadotte breaks in: "Your brothers founded it!"

Bonaparte is still loath to take offence, and replies: "Well, well, General, I would rather live in the woods than in a State where there is no security!"

Bernadotte, mockingly: "Good God! What security is lacking to you?"

Now, Bonaparte is bout to make an angry rejoinder, but Josephine intervenes to keep the peace. And yet the hidden fact is that Josephine, is, in a sense, the cause of the dissension. For Bernadotte has married Désiree Clary, to whom Napoleon had once paid court, with whom he had not found favour when he was still obscure, and to whom he had preferred Josephine when his fortunes were on the mend. Now he can forgive neither himself nor Bernadotte. Throughout his career, Bonaparte will try, by showering benefits on her, to atone to Désirée for what she has lost by not marrying him, though it was mainly her doing that they did not become man and wife. For her sake, he continually advances Bernadotte, who no less persistently betrays him.

All that his brothers and other intimates have told him about affairs in Paris during his absence, their picture of anarchical corruption and violent impotence, fills him with forebodings and urges him to speedy action. The number of the holders of power must be reduced, and their term of office must be lengthened. The government is a plateau; it must become a towering peak. A ten years' triumvirate—that will be the best plan.

At the Luxembourg they are all uneasy, now that he is back. Everyone of the Directors mistrusts him, and each of them is suspicious of his four co-Directors likewise. Which of them is intriguing with Bonaparte? Sieyés is on friendly terms with Lucien, Barras with Josephine, Gohier with both. What about Ducos? Is General Moulin to be relied on?–Immediately after reaching Paris Bonaparte had sent Moulin a Damascus blade with a diamond-studded hilt, and Moulin could not in decency refuse the gift.

Such are the secret thoughts of the Directors. Look at Bonaparte's get-up when he first came to pay us his respects! Did anyone ever see a general in such a rig? Much more like an

—his wife has a great deal of influence over him. I should have thought I had done enough to placate him! You were there, and you know. I regret having gone so far to please him. He will have to clear out of Paris. There is no other way in which I can pay my score.... Good-night, Bourrienne. Tomorrow night we shall we shall sleep in the Luxembourg."

BOOK THREE
THE RIVER

One who thoughtfully ponders the centuries,
Surveys the whole in the clear light of the spirit;
All that is petty has vanished from sight;
Oceans and continents alone are of account.

—GOETHE

Nevertheless, the great blow seems to him a questionable success. When, in the middle of June, he attacks the Austrians in the plain, the enemy, whose forces greatly outnumber his, drives him back. Where is Desaix with the promised reserves? The affair begins to have the look of a general rout. The commander, by the roadside, flicks the dust nervously with his riding-whip, as he watches the beaten army pass by. "Stand firm! Wait a little! Reinforcements are coming! Only an hour!" But the flight continues. Has fortune, too, been routed? At length Desaix arrives, and hurls himself on the dismayed Austrians; the dragoons charge; the enemy's lines are broken. The battle of Marengo, which Bonaparte had lost at five o'clock, was won by Desaix at seven—but Desaix fell in the hour of triumph.

Sad at heart, Napoleon remained on the field of battle, The best of his generals was dead; but an even more painful thought was that Desaix, not himself, had won the victory. He himself had been defeated. Maybe he was consoled by the knowledge that he alone had designed the whole campaign, and that he alone was responsible for the plan of battle in accordance with which Desaix had arrived in time to snatch success out of the jaws of failure. Perhaps he realised that this great battle, which opened and closed the campaign, had been won by him no otherwise than the Eighteenth Brumaire. Then, also, he had lost the day, and the crown of victory had been gained for him by another!

Yet in neither case can this judgment be maintained when all the circumstances are reviewed. Only three or four miles from the spot where this evening he dictates to Bourrienne the report of the battle, is the point on the map into which, four months earlier, he had thrust a pin, saying (to this same Bourrienne): "Crossing the Alps at the Great St. Bernard, I shall fall upon Melas, cut off his communications with Austria, and meet him here in the plains of the River Scrivia at San Giuliano"

This was no time for reminiscences! Statesman as well as commander, he was already parleying with Vienna, acting on the principle: "We must fight and negotiate at the same time." Now, on the battle-field, he writes again to Emperor Francis:

"The cunning of the English has neutralised the effect which my simple and frank advances must otherwise have had on Your Majesty's heart. War has become actual. Thousands of Frenchmen and Austrians are no more. —The prospect of the continuance of such horrors is so great a distress to me, that I have decided to make another personal appeal to you.—On the battle-field of Marengo, amid grief and pain, surrounded by fifteen thousand corpses, I implore Your Majesty, it behooves me to give you an urgent warning. You are far from the scene, and your heart cannot be so deeply moved as mine is on the spot. You rule over many State. -Let us give our generation peace and tranquillity. If the men of later days are such fools as to come to blows, they will learn wisdom after a few years' fighting, and will then live at peace one with another.

This long letter, of which only a few of the most weighty sentences have been quoted here, is as brilliant as had been his plan for the battle of Marengo, and it was as fruitful as his victory. For the first time it gave plain expression to his longing for peace. In days to come, he will write half a dozen such letters after as many decisive victories. Is Bonaparte, the great military commander, a pacifist after all?

By no means, but he is not a swashbuckler either. His nerves always remain sensitive to the impressions of the battle-field; and he has an unfailing reserve of scepticism as regards successes won merely by the sword. He is fond of camp life, and he has a chessplayer's love for the great game of war; but, before all, he is a statesman. It was in this very plain of Lombardy that the sense of statecraft first awakened in him. It was there that, with kings and countries as pieces, he began to play that other great game of chess, the diplomatic game. Delight in the use of spiritual force has taken possession of his soul. He will never renounce the sword, will never allow its edge to become blunted. It is as the wielder of the sword that he is acclaimed as the hero of Europe. But he also has the Golden Goblet, and does not wish to risk it anew every year.

Sound reasoning, appropriate measures. But the spirit of free thought stands weeping at the door; her fascinated gaze is fixed upon power enthroned.

V

The man who was certainly in part responsible for the before-mentioned pamphlet, perhaps its author, the man who had thus inflicted a grave injury upon the First Consul, was the very man who had been his main buttress on the Eighteenth Brumaire, and who had saved the situation that day– Brother Lucien. The most gifted of Napoleon's four brothers, six years younger that the Consul, scaling the heights of ambition at an even earlier age than his great brother, though helped in his upward progress by that brother's prestige, Lucien coveted the highest for himself. To stand in the shadow of Napoleon's great name, to be under his protection, and even to be the object of his love—these were more galling to Lucien than Napoleon's disfavour in later days. He never forgot the incidents of the coup d'état. He had been the king-maker. How, then could he obey the man whom he had raised to the throne?

Needs must, however. Shortly after Brumaire, he becomes Minister for Home Affairs, a mere instrument of the master brain. Is it not natural that he should critically examine all that comes to him from the chief, wondering whether he can make a better job? Hostile to Josephine, he is hostile to her confidants. This brings him into conflict with Fouché, who is always ready to blame the Minister for Home Affairs for anything untoward, like the publication of the pamphlet.

By temperament, Lucien was as unscrupulous and amoral as his brother. Though very like his brother, he lacked the boldly calculating brain, and may even be said to have had semi-criminal traits beneath his smiling exterior. A Napoleon, like the other, but one degree more adventurer and several degrees less statesman. At twenty-five years of age, Lucien was powerful and yet embittered, his audacious spirit urging him to more and yet more hazardous adventures. His first wife was an innkeeper's daughter; he sold monopolies; speculated in grain; lived beyond his means, instead of setting to work; bought the finest house in Paris, furnished it sumptuously, rebuilt it, and refurnished it; gave splendid banquets, indulged in amateur theatricals, wrote verses. All these extravagances were undertaken in the half-conscious desire to eclipse his brother.

Between two such men, in such a relationship, how can a breach be avoided! Lucien taunts the Consul, saying that he, Lucien, had won the victory on the Nineteenth Brumaire. In the first flush of his wrath, Napoleon has it in mind to banish Lucien; but, in the end, he is content to deprive the young man of ministerial office. This will put a term to the monetary scandals attaching to Lucien's abuse of his position. Lucien goes to Madrid as envoy. His ability in this new post enables him to work successfully against England, and also to divert the flow of a good many millions into his own pockets. Being now a widower, he soon returns, and marries his lady love a beauty whose reputation is of the same sort as Josephine's in earlier days. The First Consul is furious, for he has been working to promote a marriage that would have brought political advantages.

Joseph, too, man of the world and good fellow, is inclining to join the ranks of the sceptics, now that, with his brother's aid, he has risen to wealth and power; he frequents Madame de Stael's circle, and speaks critically of the Consul. He is no longer content with the position of envoy in Rome, refuses the presidency of the Italian Republic and the chancellorship of the Senate; cannot forget that he is the eldest; looks upon himself as head of the family.

Louis still vacillates, the poet in his temperament taking charge from time to time. For years he is in love with one of Josephine's relatives, and has no affection for Hortense, whom he is forced to marry. Years afterwards he will sing the love of his heart.

"Hitherto I have always ruled justly. It might be to my interest to seek a divorce. But what right have I to put away a good wife merely because I have become a greater man than I was when we married? She would have followed me into exile or imprisonment. Now I am to divorce her? I am not strong enough to do that. A human heart beats in my bosom; my mother was not a tigress." After Josephine's death, he would be free to choose a new partner. But, as things are, what will be the best way of solving this problem of the succession? "My brothers, like myself, were born in petty circumstances, but they did not force themselves upwards unaided as I did. The man who is to rule France must either be born to greatness, or he must be one of those whose inborn strength enables them to distinguish themselves from the herd."

In this last idea is implicit the disastrous error which in due time is to lead him to inevitable destruction.

For the nonce, however, all is done quietly and soberly, just as on two previous occasions. Wishing to be independent of the parties and to stand above them, he again demands a popular vote; and the very Frenchmen who twelve years earlier had destroyed, not only the king, but kingship, now re-establish both, doing this with even more enthusiasm than when, two years before, they had made Napoleon Consul for life. In a few days, everything is settled. First of all there are votes in the Chambers. In the Senate, only three adverse votes, those of personal enemies. In the Tribunate, Carnot is alone in recording his dissent, Carnot who admires Napoleon, but is a far-sighted devotee of the principle of freedom. The result of a plebiscite is overwhelmingly in favour of the adoption of the imperial title with hereditary succession. In May 1804, the new constitution is promulgated. It is short and businesslike, as if it were a mere paragraph modifying an old constitution. He never affects to believe that his power has a mystical origin, or even that it really springs from the people. See him, a few days after he has been proclaimed Emperor, seated in a bow window one evening after dinner. He is astraddle on a chair, with his chin resting on the back. For a long time he is silent while Josephine and Madame de Rémusat are talking (the latter records the incident). Then he stands up, turns to Madame de Rémusat, and, after posing for a while as an easygoing and cheerful man of the world, of a sudden, with that free gesture which always amazed his associates and still amazes posterity, he tore off the veil, disclosed his motives, expounded his thoughts as if he had been writing a predecessor's history:

"You were all very angry with me about the execution of the Duke of Enghien. You seem still to be fond of traditional memories. My own memory goes back only to the time when I began to be something. What is a Duke of Enghien to me? An émigré, more important than the others, and therefore one whom it is all the better to destroy.... Two years ago, power dropped into my hands in the most natural way in the world.... It is true that the Duke compelled me to cut the crisis short. I had expected to carry on the Consulate for another two years, although its forms conflicted with the reality of things. France and I could have walked along arm-in-arm for a while longer, for France had confidence in me, and wanted everything that I wanted . But after this conspiracy, which has to set the Continent in motion, it was necessary to show Europe the error of her ways...."

"The political parties I wished to conciliate, the royalists and the Jacobins, will not lose heart as long as they have somebody to dread. I realised, therefore, that no pact between them could be concluded, but that it would be possible to conclude one with them to my own advantage.... Now, they have been reduced to silence. Still opposed to me are the republicans, the cranks who believe that Europe will look on quietly while a republic is being established upon the ruins of monarchy.... That is why I preferred the imperial dignity to the dictatorship, for in an empire people no longer feel that they are travelling in unmapped country....

"You will soon see what a lure court etiquette will exercise on the émigrés. The old familiar forms of address will win over the nobility.... You French love monarchy. It is the only form of government which really suits you. I will wager, Madame de Rémusat, that you feel hundred times more at ease now that you call me 'Sire' and I address you as 'Madame' ... Your vanity was

control. When, a year after his coronation as emperor, he crowns himself in Milan with the iron crown of the Lombards (for the border States, like France itself, are to become monarchies), his voice reverberates through the cathedral as he thunders the traditional formula of the Carlovingian kings: "God gave it to me, woe to him who touches it!" Of course, it is only the statesman who speaks, for sound political reasons saying something he does not believe. But, though he is well aware of the contradiction, he will not always be able to solve it with the same vigour as in Notre Dame.

In the first place, the new position makes it necessary to impose new fetters on the mind. The Ministry of Police is revived; and France is parcelled out into four great sectors, in which the most trusty members of the Council of State, each with an army of spies, keep watch upon the mood of the country, for he wants to collect "moral statistics." Fouché is reappointed Minister of Police, and, since Napoleon's ties with Talleyrand become increasingly close, the Emperor is by degrees enmeshed in the nets of the two great intriguers-though he is aware that they are playing a double game between himself and the Bourbons, and, by a second relay of spies, fruitlessly endeavours to keep watch and ward over his watchers.

Sinister figures, these two ex-clerics, whom he hates, who hate him, but whom he will never be able to shake off.

Fouché is a man of humble origin, pale, with a cold manner, taciturn, parchmenty. Tough orders flash on his breast and a lace ruffle waves there, were it not for his piercing eyes he would look like a mummy in court dress.

Talleyrand is in all respects the man of noble birth. Lame though he be, the prettiest women pay court to him. His charm is that of a rolling sphere, whose living summit is everywhere and nowhere. The assertion that he betrayed his master only for the sake of France, is belied by his immeasurable avarice and venality. For the nonce, he continues to serve the Emperor; but, from the first, the two men have mistrusted one another. Once, indeed, Talleyrand made a sacrifice for Napoleon. Late in the evening, when the two were on a journey together, the Emperor summoned the minister to his bedside for a talk about public affairs. Suddenly Napoleon fell asleep, and Talleyrand sat on guard till morning, not stirring, lest he should wake his maker. That is his version of the affair. But the man's whole nature is so remote from any idea of sacrifice or sympathy, that we may suppose rather that his motive was the hope that Napoleon might reveal some important secret by talking in his sleep.

A dozen times every year, the name of Madame de Staël crops up. Afraid of her and her works, he keeps her away from Paris with an obstinacy which arouses wonder. Yet she says of him: "His look grows infinitely tender when he speaks to women." Throughout Europe, the champion of the freedom of the spirit fall away from him; Byron, who had greatly admired him; Beethoven, who cancels the original dedication of the *Eroica* to Napoleon. With painfully mixed feelings the Emperor must have read the tribute of the mad Tsar Paul, who had already acclaimed the First Consul as the suppressor of the revolution.

Since Marengo, he has been doing his utmost to maintain peace on the Continent, and for four years he has been successful. His hope is that the re-establishment of monarchy will appease the united princes will assuage the anger they still cherish against France. The death of two men comes to thwart his plans. Tsar Paul is murdered, and this enemy of England is succeeded by a youthful son, an idealist trained by French apostles of the enlightenment, a man with democratic leanings gentle, muddle-headed, animated by the wish to be a better sovereign. Alexander, therefore, quickly comes to an understanding with England, where, after Fox's brief predominance and death, a transient attempt at peace with France has been followed by a revival of the old jealous enmity. England fails to evacuate Malta as has been arranged, imposes new conditions, and is the first to break the peace. Once more there arises the menace of a European coalition under English leadership, a coalition that will aim at a Bourbon restoration, for talent enthroned in France sets so dangerous an example to all other countries.

None of the clan are equal to the occasion. King Joseph, in his first proclamation, compares the love of his subjects (who have never clapped eyes on his till yesterday) towards himself with the love of the French towards their emperor. He covers himself with ridicule, and makes the Emperor furious. King Louis utters, piteous sighs because the war with England forces him to interfere with "his country's" trade; and he sends, instead of troops, long letters to the Emperor filled with complaints. "Really, you are throwing unnecessary burdens upon me," replies Napoleon, in a hectoring tone. "it is all due to your narrow-mindedness and your lack of interest.... I wish you were not always whining! ...Leave wailing and complaining to women; a man must be determined.... You are governing far too gently. You allow me to bear the full brunt of the war expenses.... See to it that you raise an army of thirty thousand men. You only think of yourself; that is neither good nor magnanimous.... More energy!"

Elise, who dominats her husband, gives a constitution to Tuscany, holds reviews of the troops, changes her favourites every quarter, and amuses Napoleon by an assumption of the imperial style: "My people is content; the opposition is crushed; your commands, Sire, have been carried out. I am much pleased with the Senate; it is showing deference to my authority."

Murat, for excess of zeal, draws upon himself a reprimand phrased with Napoleon's customary bluntness: "I have seen decrees issued by yourself which are quite senseless. You seem to have lost your reason! ... All you appear to have in mind is to reign and nothing more!'

Pauline, however, is immorralised by Canova, in a work which outlasts all the realms Napoleon has set up.

Young Jerome, who has gone to America in his capacity of midshipman, has meanwhile married a lady of the middle class without consulting his family. The Emperor, who has more crowns to dispose of than siblings to give them to, and cannot spare any of his brothers, is outraged by this marriage. He persuades his mother to utter a prohibition. When the young man's ship puts in to Lisbon, the vessel is surrounded; Jerome alone is permitted to land. Bidding the lady farewell, the youthful husband swears everlasting troth; he travels alone to Paris; is received by the Emperor with threats and lures; at length he gives up his spouse for the sake of princely honours and a post as admiral; maybe, even, he will become a king. The wife fruitlessly endeavours to land on the Continent; she journeys to England, where she brings a child into the world. There she meets Lucien, her companion in misfortune. He has been well received by the English, and settles in the island realm with his wife and children. He writes poetry. An epic. What is it called?

Charlemagne

The only member of the family who is active, loyal, and, for the most part, judicious in his undertakings is Napoleon's step-son Eugene. The Emperor loves him, publicly praises his work whenever possible, and now, when Eugene becomes Viceroy of Italy and spouse of the Bavarian Princess, Napoleon writes: "You are working too hard, dear son. That is all very well for yourself, but you have a young wife who has hopes.... Why do you not go once a week to the theatre and occupy the royal box? ... One can accomplish much business in a short time. I am leading the same kind of life as yourself, but my wife is getting on in years—also I have more business to deal with!" To his step-daughter-in-law, from whom he categorically demands a male heir (seeing that Hortense's son has but one life, and the dynasty needs additional safeguards!), he writes: "Do not give us a daughter, please! Here is a recipe for you: drink some undiluted wine, daily—only you'll never believe me!" When, in his despite, she gives birth to a daughter, he says: "If one begins with a daughter, one is destined to have a dozen children!"

How marvellously Napoleon, the great stylist, can accommodate his tone to every circumstance—to inspire dread or to flatter, to praise, to spur on, to punish, or to persuade. He pours this out upon a family which is ever acting in opposition to him, and expends himself thus in the interludes of all his other business.

The Emperor's mother lives in Paris, as retired a life as her

campaigner's life, his farewell to his Polish inamorata is an au revoir.

Now Russia is open to him for the first time, a land like the desert. Endless steppes, covered with snow or mud; no bread and hardly any roads. After a few skirmishes, the Tsar slowly retreats. Can we follow him? Whither is he enticing us? Who will feed the army? There is nothing in this land to be seized, nothing such as there is in prosperous Germany, no storehouses. Had not a few hundred Polish Jews, shrewd speculators, seen the chance of striking good bargains, the regiments would have perished, at this early date, in the year 1807. When the Emperor, whose carriage has perforce been left behind, is riding towards Pultusk, he hears murmurs from the ranks. This is a soul he has almost forgotten; he heard it for the first and last time eight years ago at Acre. His generals desert, to become marauders. The Emperor is dumbfounded at the news, but what can he do? "I know my Frenchmen," he says. "It is difficult to march them on distant expeditions. France is too beautiful."

It is not surprising, therefore that when he compels the Russians to fight, for the first time he should fail to conquer in the open field. He is not actually beaten at Eylau, but both the contending armies sustain terrible losses, and the issue is indecisive. A first warning not to campaign against Russia! Report after the battle; the soldiers are rifling the potato clamps for food, and the horses are tearing straw from the roofs. The whole countryside is filled with invalided soldiers, and none of the colonels know how many men are left in their commands. The Emperor speaks:

"We shall stay here a couple of days more, and then withdraw a few miles. Post guards on all the bridges over the Vistula; no one must be allowed to cross, except the amputated. Don't bother about stragglers; no punishments." But these signs of the disintegration of his army trouble him more than in former days. A cramp of the stomach, from which he has already suffered at times, becomes more frequent, and he says: "I bear within me the germs of an early death, and shall die of the same trouble as my father." Cancer is the family heritage; his grandfather, his father, his uncle, Lucien, and Caroline, all perished of this disease.

He writes to his brother: "We are living here amid snow and mud, without wine, bread, or brandy." But this is a private missive. From Osterode, where he is housed in a barn among the soldiers, and eats whatever they can shark up for him (a comrade among his men, as he had been years before in Italy), his bulletins to Paris speak of a great victory, and of a Russian rout. The casualties are stated at a third of the true figures. The French army is in fine case, and can stay where it is for a year if thought best.

For the second time he must learn that his nerves are not made for waiting. Here, as in Egypt, this commander finds that there is something uncanny about standing still. Only once more in the whole course of his fifteen years as a conqueror will there be another such pause of two or three months in a place far from Paris. Both these epochs of tedious consideration, cautious negotiation, are filled out in the interludes of work by giving free rein to his pent-up emotions. They are filled out with idylls.

Finckenstein, a fortified Prussian castle, is now the scene of his activities, while he is awaiting the thaw on the roads and in the hearts of his adversaries. There are huge fireplaces, which are a delight to him, "for I love to look into the fire at night when I can't sleep." The place is roomy enough to house the envoys and couriers. For ten weeks, the world is ruled from here. In the great bedroom upstairs, he has had his iron camp-bed set up beside the huge four-poster.

No one knows that the Polish countess occupies the nest room—or hardly any one except Constant, his valet, and Rustam, the Mameluke. She rarely goes out, and then only after dark. The time is passed in embroidery, reading, and waiting, until the door opens, and he enters, to devote himself to her for a time. He has his meals with her alone. In these two rooms are the commander's headquarters, and here the Emperor has enshrined his idol. There are no dynastic wishes to trouble him as in Paris, no jealousies, and no bargainings for jewels; there is no wish to shine; nothing

He has periods of gloom like those from which he suffered in youth, speaks of the roaring of the sea and the moaning of the wind, has the candles shaded when he is listening to the mournful songs of Italian singers. None of his associates understands these moods; they do not realise that now, when the dream of his fancy is being fulfilled, he cannot but be disillusioned by the fulfilment, which comes otherwise than he had dreamed, and far too slowly. "You are just like all the rest of them," he says roughly to one of his ministers who congratulates him on the treaty of Tilsit. "I shall not be master until I have signed the peace of Constantinople!"

Worldwide power! Asia! These are the thoughts that continue to pulse in his brain. If he, who is always studying the tragical figures of the heroes of antiquity in search of his own image, could find the true reflexion of his own soul, it would be in the verses at this time being written by a German poet to describe the inner aspect of the Faustian unrest which he, the Emperor, with over more violent blows, is now producing in the countries of Europe.

But these dark hours are followed by others in which his mind recovers the wonted clarity of its calculations. Thus, to the tsar, the other ruler of vast territories, he writes this imaginative programme:

"An army of fifty thousand Frenchmen and Russians, with perhaps a few Austrians, could march to Constantinople, and thence hurl itself upon Asia. Once it had reached the Euphrates, England would lie at the feet of the Continent.... Within a month of our coming to an understanding, our armies can be at the Bosphorus: the influence will make itself felt as fat as India.... Of course the arrangements could only be concluded in a personal interview with Your Majesty. Everything can be signed and sealed before the middle of March. By May 1st, our troops will be in Asia, yours in Stockholm. England will collapse beneath the weight of the events with which the atmosphere will be charged. It is true that Your Majesty and I have proposed to enjoy peace within our far-flung empires.... But it is always wise and politic to do what destiny commands.... That will make this crowd of pygmies bow their heads, the pygmies who cannot see that the prototype of the present age must be sought in the remote periods of history, and not in the newspaper articles of the century that has just closed.... In these few lines I am pouring out all my soul before Your Majesty."

All his soul? Part of it, since the jewels are cut for the delectation of a muddle-headed idealist whose own dreams will be reflected with rainbow tints from their sparkling facets. But the undertaking has its elements of well-considered realism. At about this time he has an interview with a general who has been in India. This expert declares the scheme practicable, and the Emperor's hesitations superfluous. Thereupon, the latter repeatedly strokes his visitor's face with both hands, and "bubbles over with an almost childlike joy."

Thus imaginative was Napoleon.

The present leads him once more to the shade of Charlemagne. The previous year he had thought of visiting Rome to have himself crowned Emperor of the West. The Pope was to lose all temporal authority, and to content himself with a few millions as revenue; but the cardinals had vetoed the scheme. Thereupon he had rancorously exclaimed: "The whole of Italy will be subject to my laws. I will not disturb the independence of the Holy See, if Your Holiness will pay me the like consideration in temporal matters. No doubt Your Holiness is sovereign in Rome, but I am Emperor of Rome." This threatening demeanour, this Carlovingian defiance, is in sharp conflict with the constitutional law on which his power is assumedly based. In Rome, as in India, he aims at the forcible realisation of things which only the vision of his great forerunners created.

More and more frequent become the signs which show that Napoleon's historical fantasies are tending to outsoar the limits which, were he still an accurate calculator, he would regard as attainable—and terrible will be the ultimate result.

In Rome, for the time being, he is still the stronger; but so much has the habit of command grown upon him, so overweening

fashion. Besides, she grows more lovely day by day. Josephine is ageing, and is greatly distressed about a divorce."

Lucien pricks up his ears. Napoleon goes on as if he were talking at random:

"Can you believe it? She always bursts into tears when her digestion is a little upset, for she fancies she is being poisoned by those who would like me to marry someone else. That is despicable. Still, in the end, I shall have to get a divorce. I ought to have taken the step long ago, and I should have had quite big children by now; for, I may as well tell you" –he speaks earnestly–"people are wrong in thinking it is my fault we have no children. I have several. Two I know of for certain." He mentions, without naming her, Léon's mother; and then, wonder of wonders, the Polish countess. "She is an exquisite woman, an angel.... You laugh to see that I am in love. Yes, I really am; but I never forget considerations of policy. She wants me to marry a princess. Of course, as far as feelings go. I would much rather raise my beloved to the throne. You, in your dealings with your wife, ought in like manner to be guided by considerations of policy!"

"Sire, I should act as you are doing if my wife were only my mistress."

The Emperor grows more and more animated, speaks of a fixed intention to get a divorce; deplores having given the Bavarian princess to Eugene, who does not care for her and did not choose her for himself; remarks that he might long since have had Lucien's daughter betrothed to the prince of Asturia "or some other great prince, perhaps even a great emperor.... Your divorce would have to precede mine, or be simultaneous. Then there would be less chatter about my divorce; for yours, in view of your obstinate refusal for so long previously, will certainly arouse more interest. Will you do me this service? I think you really ought to."

Lucien looks at him so quizzically that the Emperor is amazed, eyes his brother up and down, and says: "Why not?"

Lucien smiles at the unreasonableness of the demand. Napoleon is embarrassed, but returns to the charge. Suddenly he addresses his brother as "my dear President" (Lucien having long ago been president of the Council of Five hundred) and adds with emphasis: "Service for service, of course — and this time you will not find me ungrateful!"

Lucien sank "into a sort of reverie, which was by no means unpleasant," so that for a few moments he hardly noticed what Napoleon was talking about. Before long he realised that the Emperor was saying, confidentially, that his only reason for wanting Lucien's divorce was that this would probably minimise the effect of his own on public opinion. Lucien, as tactfully as he could, alluded to his own advantages, pointing out that his wife was a young woman and was not barren. Napoleon took no offence. "Your wife, oh yes, your wife, didn't I tell you? She will become the duchess of Parma, your eldest boy will be her heir, without having any claim of succession to your rights as a French prince. For this is only the first stage to which I shall raise you, until something better can be found: an independent crown."

At the word "independent," Lucien cannot restrain a smile, for he is thinking of the part his brothers have to play. Napoleon notices the expression on his face.

"Yes, independent. You will know how to reign.... You need only take your choice!" His eyes flash fire, and he bangs the enormous map with the flat of his hand. "I'm not talking at random. All this belongs to me or soon will. Even today, I can do what I please. Would you like to have Naples? I will take it away from Joseph.... Italy, the loveliest jewel in my imperial crown? Eugene is no more than viceroy: He hopes to become king, expects to outlive me, but he will be disappointed in this matter. I shall live to be ninety, for I cannot do with less than that for the complete consolidation of my empire. Besides, Eugene will not suit me in Italy, after I have divorced his mother. Would you care for Spain? Do you not see that it is ripe to fall into my hands, thanks to the blunders of the Bourbons you are so fond of? Would you not like to be king in the country to which you went as envoy? What would you prefer to have? It is for you to say. Anything and everything is

When fundamental principles are under discussion, Talleyrand is apt to become more communicative: "It seems to me that Austrian policy is also that of the new regime, and I venture to say it ought to be your own policy. People count on you, Sire, to safeguard civilisation"

"Civilisation! ..." Napoleon halts in front of the fireplace and, with a sudden change of tone, says softly: Do you know why no one will negotiate with me plainly and straightforwardly? Because I have no children.... That is the secret, People are afraid of me, and everyone wants to snatch what advantages he can. This is an unfortunate state of affairs for the world, and it must be alerted."

A few days pass. Intercourse between the two rulers seems more cordial; etiquette has been forgotten; they come and go freely, like ordinary friends in private life. Napoleon spreads his nets cunningly. He says to the tsar: "Yes I need rest; I need a home. How can one get these when one has to children? My wife is ten years older than I," he goes on, falsely adding four years to Josephine's tale. "Please excuse me. What I have just said may sound rather absurd, but I do not wish, where you are concerned, to hide the stirrings of my heart." A pause. "Hullo, I see it's almost dinner time, and Baron Vincent is still waiting my leave to depart."

The kings of the drawing-room are fond of describing Napoleon as a man of camps; but how prettily he can introduce a delicate topic just before dinner, so that he can slip away without having it discussed at this state. Late that evening he summons Talleyrand to his bedside; orates, questions, suggests combinations, and issues orders by turns. At length he speaks of divorce. "Fate constrains me to it, and it is essential to the tranquillity of France, I have no successor. Joseph is a man of no account, and his children are all girls. I must found a dynasty, and my consort must be the daughter of a great line. Alexander has sisters, and one of them is of suitable age. Have a talk with Romanzoff. When the Spanish affair is settled, I shall discuss the partition of Turkey. Tell him this, and use other arguments as well. I know you have long been in favour of the divorce."

Next day, Talleyrand broaches the topic with the tsar, who has been influenced by the suggestion the Emperor has instilled with his assumption of melancholy overnight. "No one fully understands the man's character," says Alexander, much moved "All the commotion he spreads abroad is an inevitable outcome of his position. No one realises how good he is. You know him so well. What is your opinion?"

Talleyrand has no intention of saying what he really thinks, but deems it expedient, at this juncture, to let Alexander know what Napoleon had let fall about the Russian princes. "I should have no objection," rejoins the tsar promptly, "but I cannot dispose of my sister's hand without my mother's consent."

Thereafter, a long conversation between the emperors, and a renewal of intimacy; Alexander spends some more evenings with Talleyrand, talking over the teacups–but no conclusion is reached. The expanded treaty of alliance between the emperors is not signed at Erfurt, nor is the marriage to Alexander's sister arranged. Although Napoleon receives more adulation than ever before, he is disappointed at having to leave without his treaty and without his Russian bride. The only one who brings home substantial advantages is Talleyrand, for he has secured the new niece's millions.

Meanwhile the thirty-eight princes have been cajoled or threatened, rewarded or ignored, by the Emperor and his train. "In Erfurt," writes Talleyrand, "not a man among them was bold enough to face the lion.... On the last day he was surrounded by princes whose armies he had seized or destroyed, whose States and existence he had curtailed, but not one of them ventured even to proffer a request. The only wish of them all was to be seen; and to be seen last if possible, in order to remain in his memory."

In any case, Napoleon thinks Vienna will believe that to have been settled which unfortunately has not been settled. Fear will achieve what he has failed to secure through a treaty. He does not know that Talleyrand has betrayed him to Metternich, saying: "It rests with you to restore your relationships with Russia to the intimate footing that existed before Austerlitz. Nothing but an

of Lannes' soldierly judgment: when Talleyrand is kicked from behind and one is conversing with him at the moment, not a sign of his feelings can be detected in his face! Ere long he is to be seen once more, limping away from the chill festivities in the brightly lit Tuileries, following in his master's wake to resume his labours in the Emperor's study, for "he is the only man with whom I can really talk!"

Weighty matters have to be talked over. Germany has awakened; slowly she is beginning to stir; all eyes are fixed on Austria. The Prussian king hesitates as usual; and an order, dated from Madrid, has banished Baron vom Stein from Prussia. Tyrol is seething with mutiny, like Spain; Austria, now allied not only with England but also with Turkey, is arming for the fifth time. What matters it, then, that Saragossa, after a heroic struggle, should have fallen? Troops cannot be withdrawn from Spain so long as insurrection is rife. How can a war be undertaken, seeing that a vast army of a quarter million men is tied up in Spain? It is precisely on account of this situation that Austria has found courage to take up arms against the Emperor.

The Russian menace is Napoleon's last hope. When the Russian envoy, Romanzoff, is leaving for St. Petersburg, the Emperor overwhelms him with gifts and with promises. Thinking to make himself agreeable to the tsar, he pledges himself to the evacuation of Prussia; and urges Alexander, for his part, to proclaim the alliance of the two emperors to a trembling central Europe.

But Alexander vacillates; he allows himself to be reassured by Vienna, Berlin, and London; timid and hesitant as he is, he yields to the threats of his grand dukes (who to a man detest Napoleon), and yet cannot make up his mind to go whole-heartedly over to their side; Vienna's hopes of securing one of the tsar's sisters as bride for an Austrian archduke are frustrated: the tsar elects to remain neutral!

The Emperor is cut to the quick by his friend's breach of faith; indeed, it is the unkindest cut of all. He has given too much personal confidence, his pride is wounded, his labour lost. Literally, there remains nothing for him to do but to raise an army out of the very earth; the levies for the following year are now being called up, a year in advance; money must be procured by every possible and impossible means; the funds have fallen to 78, in consequence of the Spanish affair. Still, Austria is ready far earlier than he had expected. When, in April, the semaphore announces that the enemy is on the march, and Napoleon is informed of the news in his bed at ten o'clock that night, he orders the mobilization of his troops for midnight, and is furious when the unwieldy machine is not ready until four hours later.

When he arrives in Bavaria, he sees the mistakes committed by the Austrians in their advance. He can hardly believe his good luck; it was as if "he grew; his eyes gleamed, and with a delight which his glance, his mood, and his movements all betrayed, he exclaimed: 'I've got them! Their army is lost! A month hence, and I'll be in Vienna!' " He overestimates the time: he will be there in three weeks! He incites his soldiers to marches of over sixty-five miles in forty hours, and beats his foe in a series of five battles. Later he was to call these five days his finest achievement from the point of view of manœuvring. The last day he is wounded on the foot; and, since fate wills that the legend of his invulnerability (in which the army whole-heartedly believes and to which even he is inclined to lend an ear) shall be exploded, the bullet hits his Achilles' tendon.

But he speeds away again, and crosses Germany. Napoleon's carriage is outwardly plain, but within it is comfortably built. The Emperor can sleep in it; by day he can govern from it, just as well as from the Tuileries or from a tent. He is the first to overcome the friction which brings movement to a standstill; and, though he does not travel as fast as we do nowadays, he travels faster than any man ever travelled before. Five days take him from Dresden to Paris. In a number of lock-up drawers within the carriage, he collects reports, dispatches, memoranda; a lantern hanging from the roof lights up the interior; in front of him hangs a list of the

accept it, and his eighteen-year-old daughter would comply.... Acceptance is taken for granted in the first letter of his courtship, which the Emperor writes with his own hand, legibly in places, for it is penned with Méneval's aid, and with more pains than might be gathered from an inspection of the schoolboy script:

"Chère Cousine, the brilliant qualities which distinguish your person have aroused in us the desire to serve you and to honour you. Inasmuch as we are approaching the emperor, your father, with the request that he will entrust us with Your Imperial Highness' happiness, may we venture to hope that you will graciously accept the sentiments which move us to this step. Dare we flatter ourselves that you are not deciding on this step solely from a sense of duty and filial obedience?... If your Imperial Highness has no more than a trace of inclination towards us, we shall carefully cherish this sentiment, and make it our supreme task to be agreeable to you always and in all things, so that we may look forward to the happiness of winning your whole heart...."

Did ever a great genius write a more preposterous letter? He knows perfectly well that her acceptance will be dictated by filial obedience and nothing more; that she cannot possibly have a trace of liking for the devil who, during the years of her childhood, has been despoiling her father of one province after another, so that she has learned to cross herself at the sound of his name. He knows that he has better things to do, that he has other supreme tasks, than to make himself agreeable to a little goose, who is not distinguished by any other quality than by the luck of being born a Habsburg; who is neither beautiful nor wise, neither brave nor passionate. Yet the equivocal nature of his position constrains Napoleon, who has never asked a favour, to write such a letter as the foregoing!

With the gesture of a sultan, he gives to his friend Berthier (who is to woo for him by proxy in Vienna) tokens of affection for his bride: his miniature set in diamonds, and jewellery worth one-and-a-half-millions. But at the proxy wedding in the Hofburg, Napoleon is represented by the bride's uncle, Archduke Charles, whom he has worsted in a dozen battles.

as third at table. At one in the morning the whole company retires to rest. But the Emperor has taken his uncle the cardinal aside, and has asked Fesch, as an authority upon these matters, whether Marie Louise is not already his wife, thanks to the proxy marriage in Vienna. "Yes, Sire, according to civil law," answers the priest, foreseeing what is about to happen.

Next morning the Emperor has breakfast for two brought to the empress' bedside. Within an hour all Compiègne knows.

By this night attack, made on the spur of the moment, Napoleon conquers the world of legitimacy after the same fashion as he has conquered it in the field, taking the Habsburg fortress by storm, as beseems his reputation.

With a mischievous double meaning, he writes next day to his unsuspecting father-in-law: "She fulfils all my hopes, and we do not cease to give one another proofs of the tender feelings that unite us. We suit one another exceedingly well..... Allow me, therefore, to thank you for this lovely gift." Uncle Fesch does not give their union the blessing of the Church until after they have made their imposing entry into Paris. In Josephine's case, he was eight years too late; this time the sanctification has been delayed no more than a fortnight.

The Emperor finds his bride charming. "You should all marry Germans," he tells his intimates; "they are gentle, good, unspoiled, and as fresh as roses." He is delighted that she gets on well with his family. Domestic peace is new to him. He graces the intimacies of the toilet with his presence; pinches her cheeks caressingly; calls her his "bonne petite animale."

Two or three weeks later, there is news from Poland. The child conceived during the weeks at Schönbrunn has been born–a boy. There is a strange medley of feelings in Napoleon's soul. From that same Austrian palace, where he has stayed only in the absence of its rightful owner, has come the new wife, who as yet gives no signs of capacity for doing her duty. He vacillates; sends for the Polish countess. But, soon after this, Marie Louise finds that she is with child. "The Emperor's jubilation almost passes

These are nothing more than jests, but that he can find it possible to make them in a period of grave decisions indicates that there is a certain release of tension in his heavily laden heart. In truth, Marie Louise's only service to him was that during the years with which we are now dealing, her freshness did actually bring him such a solace.

But the marriage did not effect the desired release of political tension. Felix Austria, accustomed to gain advantages by these royal marriages, had hoped for a couple of provinces as dower, but had received nothing. All the more, therefore, must Emperor Francis feel rancorous on account of the humiliation inflicted upon him by the little Corsican; for, as soon as the gates of the Hofburg had closed behind Marie Louise, he could not but regard the marriage as detrimental to his dignity. To appease his legitimist misgivings, the Habsburg ruler had a search for Buonaparte ancestors made in musty old Tuscan documents, and when next he met his son-in-law was able to assure the latter that the Buonaparte lineage had been traced as far back as the eleventh century. At that time, said Francis, there had been members of the family in Treviso. Thereupon the first and last of the Buonaparti made the delicious answer:

"Thank you, Sire, I prefer to be the Rudolf of my race!"

Witty, but unwise, for such words from an upstart sovereign could not but rankle in the mind of this descendant of an ancient line! When as would soon come to pass, the question whether the emperor of Austria was to take side for or against his son-in-law was to be decided by Francis' mood, the memory of this and similar slights may have played a considerable part. Napoleon recognised this when it was too late. "Had I but made myself agreeable to that simpleton, who knows but that in the plains of Leipzig there might have been a hundred thousand fewer men in the opposing army!"

All the same, the revolutionist admired many of the ways of the legitimate ruler. One day he caught sight of a letter his wife had addressed to her father as follows: "His Sacred Majesty, the Apostolical Emperor." Napoleon considered this an excellent idea;

and in private, no doubt, his thoughts turned to Alexander of Macedon who had declared himself to be the son of Jupiter.

The apostolical emperor was especially out of humour with his son-in-law on the Pope's account. Napoleon was continually tightening the bonds round the Holy Father. Pius VII was kept at Savona. A man by no means learned in canon law, he was cut off from his advisers, and subsequently deprived of his papers, in order to make him pliable. A schism was threatening. Thirteen of the cardinals had failed to put in an appearance at the Emperor's wedding, for the Pope would not recognise the divorce which Fesch had pronounced. Now Napoleon has cases filled with the Vatican State papers brought to Paris, thus arousing the belief that he really intends to make this city the capital of Christendom; he summons a council at which the prelates of his European realm appear; he extorts a decree depriving the Pope of the investiture in case of dissent, and ultimately compels Pius to agree to this–at any rate for France.

Europe is troubled by these matters, and split into factions. On the whole, the Russians and the Poles are glad that things are going ill with the Roman pontiff; the Prussians and the English are, of course, delighted; but what arouses general surprise is that the inhabitants of the Papal States are also on the side of the Emperor. This little country, now doubly robbed of its master, is glad to accept the Code Napoleon, modern education, a rational system of administration, vigorous road construction, and the draining of the Pontine marshes. Whereas the son of the revolution has long since brought back the old spirit of Rome to Paris, he now transplants young revolutionary practice from Paris to Rome. Thus does Napoleon build bridges.

The excommunicated Emperor cunningly tries to turn the curse against the Pope. When, in newly annexed Holland, he receives the clergy in the presence of the Protestants, he rebukes the bishops as follows: "Are you of the religion of Gregory VII? I am not. My religion is that of Jesus Christ, who said: 'Render unto Cæsar the things which are Cæsar's. In accordance with the same text, I render unto God the things which are God's. I have received

as to attempt the outshining of her stepmother on these festal occasions. The empress from Paris sheds tears at the prohibition, while the empress from Vienna weeps because her pearls are smaller than those worn by Marie Louise. The old jealousies between the principalities and powers now find vent in family quarrels which the courtiers try to gloss over. When a health is drunk to the boy who should be a tie between all four of them, both the men and both the women drown their thoughts in their champagne, though each knows perfectly well what the others are thinking.

The December meeting in the windmill near Austerlitz, and the May meeting in the palace of the Saxon kings! Son-in-law and father-in-law will never set eyes on one another again.

Meanwhile, half a million men are being ranged between Königsberg and Lemberg. The master of these legions journeys to Posen, and announces the "Second Polish War," for his ostensible aim is merely to wrest Poland from the tsar–most of the old kingdom, at any rate, as far as Smolensk. "There or in Minsk." he tells a confidant, "the campaign will end. I shall winter in Vilna, organise Lithuania, and live at Russia's expense. If, then, peace cannot be secured, I shall, next year, advance into the centre of the enemy's land, and stay there until the tsar becomes pliable." The whole disposition of Napoleon's troops is made in accordance with this scheme. At Russia's expense? What supplies can he get from Russia? Has he accurate information regarding the resources of this foreign land?

In Gumbinnen, he sends for a Prussian president. Speaking of the stores of grain he has collected in the German ports, and proposes to have sent to Kovno, he says:

"I presume there are plenty of mills in Kovno?"

"No, Sire; very few mills are to be found there."

The Emperor looks at Berthier "dubiously" This glance of the supreme war lord at his chief of general staff is a foreshadowing of the disillusionments he is to experience in the unknown land beyond the Memel. It is not the mere lack of mills which disturbs him, but the fact that he is taken by surprise. For a whole year, the

Emperor has been preparing the great campaign. Troops, parks of ammunition, reserve corps, fourteen hundred pieces of ordnance, siege trains, bridge-building materials, pontoons, have been assembled from seven realms, counting the Confederation of the Rhine as one. Eight Baltic fortresses are used as storehouses, to which hundreds of ships and thousands of wagons bring wheat and rice. Some of the wagons are drawn by oxen which are destined for the slaughter house at the end of their journey—a symbol of compulsory military service, in which a man serves only that he may die. Now Napoleon learns that he is about to enter a country without mills. He can build them, no doubt; but at what cost in time and men! Are other surprises awaiting him across the Russian border? It will be impossible to carry fodder for one hundred and fifty thousand horses. That is why he has waited till June, when the grass will be green. But what if the steppe should disappoint him here?

And what if his men's spirit should disappoint him?

On the frontier, warning voices make themselves heard. He is told that these young recruits are hardly able to endure the long marches, and that the heat will be too much for them. In Dresden, Murat had vainly asked for furlough. Now, in Danzig, he and Berthier and Rapp are dining with the Emperor in gloomy silence. Napoleon, emerging from his thoughts of world conquest, suddenly asks Rapp: "How far is it from Danzing to Cadiz?" Rapp is bold enough to answer: "Too far, Sire!" thereupon the master rejoins:

"I can see, gentlemen, that you no longer have any taste for fighting. The king of Naples would rather be back in his pretty kingdom; Berthier would like to be playing the sportsman in Grosbois; Rapp would fain be enjoying the sweets of Parisian life!"

The marshals answer never a word, for they will not deny that it is so. But that it should be so, is a new experience for Emperor Napoleon.

When he reaches the Memel, the symbolic significance of the Russian frontier captivates his imagination to such an extent

scene? An officer of no account, powerless, unknown, is the representative of Holy Russia; before him, in the storied hall of the tsars, stands the mighty Emperor of the French, the conqueror at whose slightest nod all Europe trembles. The Emperor speaks, chaffers, poses conditions with this man, as though the occasion were another Tilsit and the captain the tsar.

"I am conducting a purely political war," Napoleon reiterates. "All I need is the fulfilment of our treaties. Had I taken London, I would not have offered to leave it so speedily. From here, however, I intend very soon to withdraw. If the tsar wants peace, he must let me know of his desire.... I am setting you free, but on condition that you make your way to St. Petersburg. The tsar will be glad to see an eyewitness of recent happenings in Moscow. You must tell him everything."

"I shall not be permitted to enter his presence, Sire"

"Appeal to Court Chamberlain Tolstoy. He is an upright man. If he fails you, get the tsar's body servant to introduce you to his presence, or you must approach His Majesty during one of his daily walks...." The captain gets cold all over; it seems to him that he is being urged to commit a crime, an attempt on the tsar's life. He can promise nothing; stammers.

The Emperor says: "Very well. I shall write a letter to your emperor and you must see that he gets it." This last missive, which finds its way from one emperor's hands into those of the other, is the strangest of the trio.

"My Lord Brother.... Beautiful, magical Moscow exists no more.... This deed is loathsome, and to no purpose. Did you wish to rob me of my means of support? They were in the cellars, to which the flames never penetrated. How could you consign to destruction the loveliest city in the world, a city it has taken hundreds of years to build; how could you lay it waste for so little gain!... Out of kindness, and in the interests of Your Majesty, I have now taken charge of the town which the Russian army had sacrificed. At least the municipal authorities and the militia should have been left in the city, as was the case in Vienna, on two occasions, and in Berlin and Madrid; Milan, likewise, acted thus when Suvaroff entered at the head of his army.... It is surely impossible that you, with your high principles and your good heart, can have consented to such abominations, for they are unworthy of a great ruler and a great nation. Your people were so busy getting the fire-engines away, that they abandoned one hundred and fifty pieces of ordnance.... I have warred against Your Majesty without bitterness. A sign from you, before or after the last battle, would have stayed my forward march; nay, for Your Majesty's sake, I should have wished to forgo my entry into Moscow.... If you have presented any of your former friendship towards me, you will receive this letter favourably. In any case, you will be grateful to me for informing you of the recent occurrences."

The letter of a tutor to his pupil angry and threatening, written from the depths of his isolation, with intent to rouse the recipient. Thus might an impeccable moralist write to a ne'er-do-well! The whole epistle turns upon the two words "receive favourably"; this is the aim; on these words are built up the writer's hopes. Will the letter fulfil its mission?

The advance of the invader, the threatening proximity of the foe, the burning of Moscow, have filled all hearts in St. Petersburg with despair. The court is for peace. Can a more favourable opportunity present itself? The enemy is becoming more embarrassed day by day. Emperor Napoleon is eager for negotiations. The madcap grand duke Constantine is in favour of a parley; the tsarina-mother, she who hates the upstart, who refused her daughter to him as bride, who railed at Alexander for weeks after the Tilsit meeting, even she advises the tsar to clasp hands once more in friendship with the Emperor. Now is the time!

But Alexander held firm. Two men were responsible for his unwonted steadfastness, One was a Frenchman, Bernadotte. He and the tsar had recently met in Finland, and Bernadotte had strengthened Alexander in his determination to persevere, had even handed back the Russian auxiliary corps which the tsar had lent for the conquest of Norway. Bernadotte's hatred was so

VIII

Forty bowed backs receive the beaten war lord on his return home. The sight of the court dresses which he has embroidered with his contempt revives his belief in the folly and the weakness of these men whose only wish is to be ruled. But his glance strays to the bars of the golden cage in which the son of liberty has locked himself up. He does not realise that the people of his capital are weary and disaffected; and instead of following the example of his own youth, instead of with disarming frankness acknowledging the faults he hopes to better, he postures as Cæsar before his servile officials, and rails at the weather god, though but yesterday he had boasted his power to make what weather he pleased throughout Europe.

During the nine days' drive from Warsaw to Paris, the uncertain mood of the adventurer had given place once more to the steadily aspiring flame of the imperator. Although the Russian winter had set in later than usual, he carries off the reverse by saying: "The army sustained heavy losses, but that was because the winter began so early.... The king of Naples is not fitted for high command, and he lost his head after my departure.... All the same, I have three hundred battalions left, without bringing a single man back from Spain."

Has his contempt for his fellows risen to such a pitch that he can serve up these fables to experienced men who have known the truth for months? But their consciences are uneasy. They feel responsible for the October putsch, or at any rate guilty for not having made an end of the whole business within the first quarter of an hour. On the other hand the Emperor, whose own heart accuses him, is glad to play the accuser, for it galls him that in the decisive hour they should have forgotten the empress and the heir to the throne. In memorable words, at the first reception in the Tuileries, he tries to hammer his point into the heads of his councillors.

"The apostles of the rights of man are really to blame for all that had happened. They declared rebellion to be a duty. They flattered the people, imputing to it a sovereignty it is incapable of exercising. They destroyed respect for law by establishing the supremacy of an assembly which knew nothing of administration and law, instead of holding fast to the nature of things! Anyone who wishes to build up a State once more, must be guided by the very opposite principles. History depicts the human heart, and we must study history if we would learn the merits and defects of legislation.... When I undertook the reconstruction of France, my prayer was that I might be spared for a considerable number of years, seeing that what has been destroyed in a moment will take a long time to refashion. The State needs courageous officials. "The king is dead; long live the king!' That was the watchword of our fathers. The phrase makes us realise the advantages of monarchy."

Were is not for the prettily turned expression about history and the human heart. Emperor Francis might have subscribed to this speech, and it might have been an ornament to the pages of any of the familiar expositions of monarchical doctrine. Why should people go on quarrelling about such matters? The ancient dispute between tradition and revolution has been settled, now that the son of the revolution has acknowledged the supremacy of tradition. No matter whether an heir be named Bourbon or Bonaparte! When we compare the two fathers we see that they are very much alike! His marriage with the daughter of one who rules by right divine has complicated the problem, and has sophisticated his own genius.

Or does he believe no more than half of what he is saying? Before setting out on the Russian campaign, he had frankly explained his plans to Metternich: "The legislature belongs to me; all I need is to put the key of the deliberative chamber in my pocket. France is less suited for democracy than a good many countries.... When I get back, therefore, I shall transform the Senate and the Council of State into an Upper House and a Lower House, most of whose members I shall myself nominate. These

future no attention is to be paid to anything you say.... By such behaviour you may disturb the march of my whole army. It is sheer cheating!"

Soon afterwards Junot, one of the oldest of his comrades, becomes affected with megalomania; he loses a battle in Illyria, and then, in a fit of frenzy, throws himself out of a window. Bourrienne, who had for a time been cashiered on account of peculation, and had then been appointed chargé d'affaires in Hamburg, had, after all, to be dismissed once more for the old offence. "If he dares to interfere in public business, I will have him arrested, and make him disgorge his ill-gotten gains!" Bernadotte, the most faithless, has actually landed in Pomerania with his Swedes, has advised the allies to stand firm, and will deceive them as he has deceived others. To crown all a sworn enemy of the Emperor is now to join the opposing combination. General Moreau, who had been exiled to America for his share in Cadoudal's conspiracy, is on his way to join the foes of France, and will share with Bernadotte the distinction of fighting against his native land.

In this situation, on the horns of a dilemma, too cautious to turn his victories to account, and too powerful to accept the terms on which alone he would be able to make peace, the Emperor has recourse to his whilom methods. He invites Metternich to Dresden, and tries to win over the Austrian diplomat by suggestion. The interview is typically Napoleonic, lasting nine hours without a break. The Emperor gains nothing by it, but posterity gains a great deal.

Standing in the middle of the room, his sword buckled on and his hat under his arm, the Emperor receives the minister. After making formal enquiries about his father-in-law's health, he forthwith assumes the offensive: "So you, too, want war. Well, you shall have it. I have crushed the Prussians at Lützen, and have beaten the Russians at Bautzen. You are waiting for your turn? Be it so, we shall meet again in Vienna. Men are incorrigible! Three times I have replaced Emperor Francis on his throne; I have promised always to live at peace with him; I have married his daughter. Even at that time I thought: 'You are making a fool of yourself.' Still, I did it and now I regret it!"

We see that he is not disposed to be civil, that to his father-in-law's envoy, on whom he wishes to make a good impression, he is blunter than he had been to Francis on the day after Austerlitz. Metternich speaks of world peace, which will only be possible if the Emperor is willing to accept a reasonable curtailment of his dominions. It will be necessary to give back Warsaw to the tsar and Illyria to the emperor of Austria, to set the Hansa towns free, to enlarge Prussia.

"What you are asking is that I shall dishonour myself. I will die rather than cede a hand's breadth of soil. You born kings can accept defeat twenty times over, and still go back to their palaces. I am the child of fortune, and I cannot do this! My power will not outlast the day on which I cease to be strong, on which I cease to be feared.... Through the cold of Russia I lost everything except honour.... Now I have a new army; you shall see it; I will hold a review for your benefit!" Here we have once more the pride of the born soldier facing those who are born kings; here we have General Bonaparte. When the minister venturess to declare that this army of which Napoleon speaks would be glad if peace were made, the Emperor cuts Metternich short with one of his amazing outbursts of frankness:

"It is not the army that wants peace! My generals want it! Really, I have no generals left. The cold of Moscow has demoralised them all. There, the bravest among them cried like children. A fortnight ago, I could still make peace; now, after two victories, I can no longer do so."

"Europe and you, Sire, will never come to terms. When you have made peace, it has been nothing more than a truce. To you, success and failure are equally strong motives for war. This time the whole of Europe will fight against you."

The Emperor laughs savagely:

"Do you think to destroy me by a coalition? How may of you are there, then, Messieurs les Alliés? Four, five, six, twenty?

to retain her natural frontiers; the Rhine, the Alps, the Pyrenees, the Emperor feels that he is saved. Without a moment's delay he will accept the Frankfort proposal. Maret has actually drafted the dispatch.

Suddenly he changes his mind. Why? Perhaps he has been put out of temper by the opposition voiced in the Chambers. There, at length, the members are showing themselves refractory. "We will not vote further armaments unless the government agrees that they are to be used only for defence. The Emperor must pledge himself to carry out all the laws that protect liberty." Thunders of applause greet these words. For the first time in fifteen years, an assembly has ventured to criticise Napoleon. In his hatred for all Chambers, the emperor flies into a passion, forbids the printing of the speech, closes the House, receives a few of the deputies, scolds them:

"The throne is nothing more than a piece of wood covered with satin. I, and I alone, represent the people. I am the State. If France wants a different constitution, let her find another monarch for himself. Do you think my words proud? I utter them because I have the courage, and because France owes her greatness to me." After this language in the vein of the Roi Soleil, on New Year's Day he openly threatens the deputies, and says he will have them closely watched.

That very day, Blücher crosses the Rhine.

Thus, after twenty years of effort, and after six great wars, the more or less united powers of Europe and the old monarchical idea, incorporated in a Prussian field marshal, have made their way back across the boundary river of the revolution–and in the same hour, the heir of these modern ideas scatters their representatives and threatens imprisonment. With a similar logic, the manifestoes of the conflicting worlds have changed places. In Notre Dame, where for twenty years nothing has been heard but thanksgiving services, prayers are now offered up on behalf of the success of French arms. From the allies, on the other hand, who have so long heard talk of success of the French arms as heralding the liberation of conquered peoples, come assurances to conquered France that the invaders are "liberators."

The legitimists have at length learned from their great foe the technique of his battles and his proclamations. But if they are able to turn the lesson to good account, it is only because of their preponderance of power, and because of the weariness of a nation; which, after twenty years of glory, now seeks nothing but repose.

To begin with, they weaken their position by asking too much; for when they offer nothing better than the old frontiers of 1792, the Emperor breaks off negotiations, and makes ready to repel their onslaught. In spite of all difficulties, he is able to strengthen his fighting front. His spirits are now steadily rising. When a pious count advises him to send the empress and her ladies to kiss the relics of Ste. Genevieve, Napoleon bursts out laughing, and says: "You're a pretty bigot! I am going to fight it out!"

But to whom, in this stern moment, does he entrust the capital? Who merits all his confidence?

Joseph! Joseph, who understands nothing about war and has been keeping open house for the Emperor's enemies, becomes lieutenant general of France and governor of Paris! This domestic peace treaty throws a glaring light upon the Emperor's isolation, upon his lack of confidence in his supporters, and upon his family feeling. Shortly before leaving for the front, Napoleon has coldly ordered his brother to choose between openly declaring himself to be the friend of the empress-regent or continuing to be banished from Paris. "You can live in retirement at your country-seat, so long as I am alive. If I die, you will be killed or imprisoned. At Morfontaine, you will certainly be of no use either to your own people or to France, but at any rate you will not do me any harm. Make your choice. Feeling, whether friendly or hostile, are useless and out of place."

The tone is that of a man fighting to save his crown. He reckons with the likelihood of death; burns a great many State papers; and provides for his natural sons. Little Leon is to receive a fixed income, Walewska's boy is to have a big majorat. As for

"During the night they were led into the Austrian camp. They were told that they were marching against the enemy."

"My men have to be duped before they can be torn away from me! Did you see Marmont at the time he set out?"

"No, Sire."

"The cavalry, too?"

"In close columns."

"Where is Mortier?"

"He sent me to tell you that his corps will be loyal to you in life and in death. He awaits Your Majesty's orders. The young guard is ready to die for you. All young France is ready!"

The emperor steps close up to the young officer, looks him straight in the eyes, and with a friendly gesture allows his hand to slip under the fringe of the epaulette so that it may rest on the captain's shoulder. Thus does the ageing Napoleon find support once more in the young men of France.

When Caulaincourt brings the demands, he is accompanied only by Macdonald.

"Where is Ney?"

Silence. A pause. Then he is told the conditions. They probe him to the quick. To disavow the dynasty! For a decade the dynasty has been his goal.

"My personal withdrawal did not suffice? Must I, with my signature, disinherit my wife and my son? I cannot do this! I won their throne for them by my deeds!" The paradox has taken such deep root in his thoughts that he has ceased to be aware of its existence. Then he counts his troops again.

"I have twenty-five thousand men here; I can speedily bring up another eighteen thousand from Italy; Suchet has eighteen thousand, Soult forty. I shall fight! ..."

The remaining troops are loyal, but the leaders are weary of the struggle. Why does he not place himself at the head of his guards? Because he can only think in terms of marshals, because the feudalist atmosphere is cutting him off from his stalwarts.

Here they all come again! They warn him, even Berthier

joins with the others now, that Fontainebleau can easily be surrounded. He listens to them with dignified composure. Then he abruptly asks them whether they are prepared to march with him to the Loire; or to Italy, where they can join Eugene's forces. Behind the proposal, we sense new plans of our adventurer. But the men who stand before him are marshals and Frenchmen; they breathe the words "civil war", they advise him to abdicate. The island of Elba has been chosen for his dwelling place; he had better take what he can get! He dismisses them.

"None of them has either heart or reins! I am not so much beaten by fortune, as by the ingratitude of my brothers-in-arms. It is infamous. All is over!"

Without, in the drawing-room, groups of courtiers and dignitaries have assembled. Voices are hushed as though a king lay dead. All are awaiting the signature. The Emperor is well aware of this, he allows no one to enter his room, he will keep them waiting till morning. After a feverish, sleepless night, his negotiators find him sitting in his dressing-gown before the fire, a broken man and pitiable.

They bring him the deed which they have signed in Paris that night. He is to receive Elba, and two million francs as annual subsidy; he is to retain the title of Emperor; he is to have a guard of four hundred men. Talleyrand had warned the allies that this proximity of the lion to France was a menace; he suggested Corfu, and even mentioned St. Helena. Fouché endeavours to shield the Emperor from a slow descent from the heights; in elegantly phrased letters he suggests that Napoleon should go straight to America, where, as a free citizen, life could be started anew. –The farther away from the coasts of Europe, the better!

All this leaves the Emperor cold. He is visioning something different. He sees how Macdonald is standing the test; in his secret heart he is comparing this marshal with those others who have shown so much ingratitude; he feels now that he has not honoured the man enough. In this hour when he has to sign his abdication, Napoleon says:

"I have not sufficiently rewarded you. Now I can do no

thus embodies the unhappy union of two antagonistic worlds, the name of Napoleon is soon destined to be heard no more. For, when the young cuckoo is introduced into the Habsburg nest, he is called Francis, and nothing else. Later, when the empress' secretary is leaving Vienna and presents himself to take farewell, the boy draws him into a window recess and says in a hurried whisper: "Tell my father I love him tremendously!"

What must be the tenor of Napoleon's thoughts when he hears gossip about a certain Neipperg, and Austrian officer, a man of no account, and one whose only way into history is through the bedroom of a Habsburg princess–who would herself never have been heard of had it not been for her marriage to Napoleon. Thus terrible are the blows of fate, and his intimates think it natural enough when they see their master weeping over his boy's portrait.

But now Pauline arrives, fascinating as ever, in the best of spirits. To amuse him, she mimics the grimaces that are made by the worthies of the island and their wives when, at the weekly receptions, the Emperor asks them how many children they have, and whether they think he ought to build a hospital. As the year draws on, Italians from the mainland come in increasing numbers. Persons with satisfactory recommendations–historians, poets, men of birth, and even Englishmen–secure a good reception; and he will talk to them for hours, though only of the past, with never a word about the future. He is delighted to hear such visitors rail at the Austrian regime which has now been set up once more, but he will pay no heed to conspirators who wish him to come to Italy as leader of a revolt. His thoughts range towards the other coast, and by slow degrees mature into plans.

What is Paris saying?

To him this is still the question of questions. The news brought to him in the journals twice a week, and the information he gleans from his visitors, lead him to turn new possibilities over in his mind. But it must not be supposed that Napoleon began the new epoch with a definite plan. When he landed in Elba, it was an open question in his mind whether he would ever quit the island. Still, the thought of future possibilities was intensified in him by the usual foreboding of an adventurer–the adventurer he had become since the failure at Moscow. "A living drummer is better than a dead emperor." Slowly, as the conditions change, he makes plans and rejects them, renews and modifies his designs. They turn upon what is happening in Paris and in Vienna.

What is Paris saying about the Bourbons? Hardly is Napoleon away, when they make their "entry" after the usual manner of exiled kings who return; and through the newspapers, under duress of the censorship the Emperor had established, lie like troopers, in his remote island he can learn the ridiculous truth. Four persons are sitting in a small carriage. The Parisians, whose risibilities are easily touched, certainly have something to laugh at. The king is there, in an amazing rig-out, in plain clothes, but decked with gigantic epaulettes; a man so fat that he has three chins, and he smiles at the gaping crowd. Beside him is the duchess of Angoulème, her face tearful with reminiscence. On the opposite seat are the prince of Condé, a very old man, and the duke of Bourbon; they wear the uniforms of the good old days, which none of the younger onlookers have ever seen before. This carriage, freighted with the resurrected ghosts of those who had been laid to rest twenty-two years ago, was attended by Emperor Napoleon's sulky-looking guard, men whose uniforms, shot and slashed, bore witness to the titanic struggles that had been waged in the interim.

The Emperor makes eager enquiries concerning the habits of his successor on the throne, and is gratified to learn that Louis has taken over his room without making any changes. The king's demeanour is said to be far from regal. According to a German description of this date, Louis was "extremely obese, so fat that he can hardly walk. Wearing black satin boots, he is supported on each side, and would stumble over a straw. He is clad in a sort of blue soutane with a turn-over red collar and hanging golden epaulettes of an antique pattern." This sort of thing keeps the Emperor amused for a whole hour. For a dozen years, England has keen publishing caricatures depicting Napoleon's camp manners in the palace of the Bourbons, and now this legitimate ruler, set up

answer to that hour when Napoleon had had to choose between the mother's life and the child's, and had decided in favour of the mother. Not until his wife has cast her vote against him, is the Emperor made an outlaw: "The powers declare that Napoleon Bonaparte has placed himself outside the bounds of civil and social relationships, and that as an enemy and disturber of the peace of the world he is consigned to public prosecution."

The tidings leave him unmoved. He is used to being outlawed. When he left Corsica, he and all his relatives were under sentence of outlawry. The word "outlaw" had been shouted at him in the Orangerie at Saint-Cloud. The Pope had pronounced the major excommunication against him. All three anathemas had glanced harmless from his coat of mail, so that he deemed himself impregnable. But this fourth ban will lay him low.

He still continues to hope in the Habsburg. Announcing his intention to summon the Electoral Colleges of the Empire to a great assembly, he speaks of the gathering, in Carlovingian terminology, as a Champ de Mai, for he intends to have the empress and his son crowned there. He thinks that this will ensure Austrian support, and writes to his wife:

"I am master of France. The people and the army are wild with enthusiasm! No one but the so-called king has run away to England.... I expect you here in April with my son." The thought of his dynasty is ineradicable.

But even this most natural of feelings assumes a distorted form, for his feelings are in pawn to the old world. Writing to the man who has just outlawed him, he says: "At the moment when providence has recalled me to the capital of my States, It is my chief desire, the object of my tenderest inclination, to see my wife and son once more." He goes on to speak of his wife, who must certainly reciprocate his longing. Then: "All my endeavours are directed towards the firm establishment of this throne which the love of my people guarantees and restores to me; and towards handing it down to my son in due time, based upon an imperishable foundation. ... Since a lasting peace is essential to the attainment of this important and sacred aim, there is nothing nearer to my heart than to remain at peace with all the powers."

Is this sublime, or is it ridiculous? Napoleon renounces war and abandons his designs on Europe. He speaks truth when he says that he needs nothing more than France. The monarchs who had conquered him last year have formed a new alliance against him, and have declared him an outlaw. The sentence of outlawry has been signed by Emperor Francis, in the Austrian capital, with Marie Louise's express authorization. She had left him after the last defeat; had thrown up the regency which she had sworn to carry on faithfully; had taken the boy with her; had thrown herself into another man's arms, and is still living with him: The Emperor knows these things. But now, instead of beginning the new era with a clear-cut severance from all that has overthrown and disappointed him, he begins by suing for the friendship of this old throne which had triumped over his new one.

This is the ban, this is the outlawry, which will for the second time bring him to his doom.

XVII

The adventurer now becomes a rat-catcher, like the Pied Piper of Hamelin. Bourbon had been clever enough to invite the best talents to serve him; and as a result of this, when once the royalist national anthem had been sung, all went smoothly for him. Some of these men know not whether to go or to stay: they wait upon events. But Napoleon, who has always commanded, who has never canvassed for anyone's services, places the flute of the tempter to his lips: he knows that now is the time for suggestion and smiles. The loyal few, he restores to their posts, with a shake of the hand. Maret, Davoust, and Caulaincourt, form part of his ministry.

He knows all that those who have proved ungrateful have been doing, and he judges them by their records. Officials, offic-

retreat from degenerating into a rout, and sends to let his ally know that they can form a junction at Wavre the next day. With an inertia which we should wonder at did we not know that Napoleon is ailing and prematurely old, the Emperor makes no move on the day after his victory. Too late he sends Grouchy with thirty thousand men to follow up the Prussians, not believing that they can reorganize their forces speedily, or that after the heavy losses they have sustained they will be able to effect a junction with the English. Yesterday, he had dealt with the Prussians singly; tomorrow he will be able to defeat the English, now cut off from their allies. His seventy thousand men will suffice. He fails to allow for Gneisenau's imperturbability and for Blücher's impetuosity.

For the first time, he underrates an opponent. At Friedland, Aspern-Essling, and Laon, he was not beaten. Nor was he beaten in Russia. At Leipzig, and at Arcis-sur-Aube, he was defeated; but it was because he had only a small army with which to meet the onslaughts of vastly superior forces; those of three great powers in one case, and those of four in the other. Never, yet, had any isolated commander been able to say: "I have defeated Napoleon."

Now he thinks too much of his victory, and too little of his opponent. For the first time he fails to focus his lens accurately, with the result that one point escapes his reckoning. But it is not that he makes a wanton and ill-considered onslaught. Nor is the trouble on this occasion that family feeling makes him entrust leadership to inefficient hands. If he had kept Grouchy's force with him, his enemy would have scarcely outnumbered him. But the course of the decisive battle shows that this error in calculation was not the main cause of the French defeat.

The final cause, as anyone can recognize who studies all the elements in Napoleon's fate, was the man's advancing years.

His activity was undermined by his ailments, and that is why, on the morning of the battle of Waterloo, he failed to attack promptly. In the middle of June, the sun is above the horizon by four. If the Prussians were able to march upon the roads that had been softened by the recent heavy rains, the French veterans could have done the same–for the Emperor's soldiers on this occasion were almost all of them tried men. But he waits till noon, that he may place his guns better when the ground becomes less sodden! At Jena, in October, in a Scotch mist, he had headed his troops, shouted to encourage them, attacking so early in the morning as to arouse many of his foes from their slumbers. Today he waits till noon.

The loss of this half-day is to destroy him. He rides to an elevation bearing the fatal name of La Belle Alliance; he arranges his troops in three lines, rides along the front, shouts to his men in metallic phrases; he is going to break through the enemy and enter Brussels; he already has the proclamation to the Belgians in his pocket. He has only wasted half a day!

In the afternoon, when battle is already joined, news comes that Bülow's corps is advancing. The Emperor turns pale and sends Grouchy orders to come back. Will the orders reach him? If they do, will he be able to disengage himself from the enemy? Everything turns upon the fortune of the next hour. The English must be beaten before the Prussians can come to their aid. Napoleon delivers a great cavalry attack on the centre, but the English stand firm. Shall he use the old guard? Not yet! Not yet! Bülow is already beginning to fire. At all costs he must keep the line of retreat open, for otherwise there may be a catastrophe. But, in fact, the English forces are already half defeated. It is five o'clock, and the guard might have finished their defeat, for at this hour Wellington sent a message to his Prussian ally: "Unless your corps keeps marching, and attacks without respite, the battle will be lost." This would have been the moment for an attack by the old guard, but once more caution makes the Emperor hold his hand at the critical moment. He sees that a second Prussian corps is about to attack.

A dread decision! A brilliant gamester staking his last coins but today he must not be beaten. At length, towards seven, he sends the last five thousand guardsmen, the veterans, to attack. Now, it is only a forlorn hope. "Vive l'Empereur!"

This cry has shaken half Europe. Is it not a century old? In

"If you had tried to escape in a French frigate," says Maitland, "you would have seen for yourself how well we can shoot."

No repining! Here stands a gamester who has lost the game. All that the Emperor troubled to dispute is Maitlands contention that two frigates with a few twenty-four pounders could not possibly have got the better of the "Bellerophon," which carried seventy-four heavy guns. The captain proves that it would have been impossible. Napoleon examines the ship's guns, praises what he sees, but has some criticisms to make here and there. Maitland declares afterwards, when alone with his own people, that he has been amazed by the extent of the Emperor's technical knowledge.

The ship puts out to sea.

Meanwhile, the legitimate ministers and kings are discussing their course. Not a single member of this circle proves great enough to advise a great gesture, before Europe and before history. Then days after leaving the roads of Rochefort, the "Bellerophon" anchors in Plymouth harbour. It is a fine morning in the end of July, and the water is thronged with rowing boats full of people anxious to catch a glimpse of the caged lion. Since no decision has yet arrived from London, civilian visitors are not allowed on board. But it is a great time for the crew. They can see Napoleon every day, and he converses with any of them that are able to speak French. The gaping crowds in the boats are the thousands who for twenty years past have heard nothing but abuse and mockery of "Boney"; have seen numberless caricatures of him, depicted as a hideous monster. Now, they are all animated with the same curiosity; they all want to feast their eyes upon this dread spectre.

For the most part, Napoleon stays in his cabin. He does not want to become a raree-show. A few days' patience, and he will be able to go ashore, and live where he pleases. At length, however, feeling the need for fresh air, he comes up the gangway and mounts the poop. There he stands, the great defeated foe, in his old world-famous green coat; defenceless. Thousands of eyes instantly converge on him, so that it seems as if he must be consumed in their fire.

But the man with the simple, impenetrable countenance, who is thus pilloried, must radiate an aura of dignity and suffering, for an extraordinary thing happens. Thousands of heads are bared. As far as Napoleon's gaze can reach, on the boats, the ships, throughout the harbour, not a man remains covered. The greeting is universal, but for one exception. Only one man among all those onlookers keeps his three-cornered hat on his head. It seems as if the whole nation were willing to pay the Emperor the homage which a pettifogging captain withheld.

Such was the judgement of the British nation, which in this tense moment cleared itself from all the contumely so soon to be heaped upon its name. The waiting lasted three days. On the fourth, British officers entered the Emperor's cabin, and laid before him a paper containing the government's decision. No direct answer had come from the prince regent.

The document was to the effect that it would not be consistent with he government's duties towards England and her allies to allow General Bonaparte any further opportunity of disturbing the peace of Europe, and it would therefore he necessary to restrain his liberty to "whatever extent may be necessary for securing that first and paramount object." St. Helena would be his place of residence, as it was healthy, and would admit of a small degree or restraint than might be necessary elsewhere. He could take with him three officers, a physician, and twelve servants.

Such was the reply of the modern Xerxes.

Napoleon, we are told, "laid the paper on the table, and, after a pause, began to protest in vigorous terms." He said:

"I am not a prisoner of war! ... I came on board the 'Bellerophon' of my own free will, after previous negotiation with the commander. I threw myself on your protection, and claimed the rights of hospitality. The tricolour was still waving over Rochefort and Bordeaux. I might have gone back to the army; or might for years have lived secretly among the people, who were devoted to me.

One of the most sublime forms of his egotism is gratitude. This is not ordinary kindness, but the pride of a man who feels he is unique, and overwhelms with benefits anyone who has ventured to be useful to him, lest he should possibly remain in the other's debt. That was the consideration which really underlay his frequently declared policy, that he would never make use of any party, lest he should incur obligations. We must not look upon these things in a romantic light. But it is an actual fact that he was not content to promote only the friends of his youth, his fellow-students at the military academy. As soon as he rose to power, he found for the priest who had been headmaster at Brienne a sinecure at Malmaison as librarian–without any books! The sometime school porter became lodge keeper at his country house. A young lady of noble birth to whom, in his lieutenant days, he had once paid court for a whole evening, and who sixteen years later applied for help to the Emperor, received what she wanted, together with a post for her brother, and a friendly letter. He remembered many of his former associates in his will. Years after his brief intimacy with "Giorgina," when he hears that she is in difficulties (though she has made no application to him), he provides her with a competency.

Hitherto we have been talking about money, or money's worth. But the nature of his gratitude is different when he loves, as in the case of Josephine. When we consider his relationships with her, we realize the truth of Marmont's tribute, which is all the more remarkable as coming from an enemy: "He had a greatful, kind, indeed affectionate, heart." At the time of the coronation, he says to Roéderer: "What right have I to put away a good wife merely because I have become a greater man than I was when we married? ... Before all, I am a just man." A little later, he writes to Josephine: "As far as I am concerned. I deem ingratitude the greatest weakness anyone can have."

III

Napoleon's self-confidence, his self-esteem, his egotism, lies at the root of his wavering between revolution and legitimacy. Relying entirely upon himself, scorning all whose pride rests upon the accident of birth, he has nevertheless to take the egotism of others into account in so far as this egotism becomes embodied in achievement. And yet he is constitutionally incapable of suffering others to be on an equal footing with himself. For his own sake he has to choose the most capable to fill administrative and other positions, and yet he has to please the masses; he must stand for equality of all, and at the same time bear the individual in mind. These contradictions give rise to a tragical conflict.

Both the weapons he has chosen for his battle of life, namely, the spirit and the sword, he conceives of in a revolutionary sense. "Why is the French army the most dreaded in the world? Because the officers became émigrés; non-commissioned officers replaced them, and became generals. One can lead a people's army with non-commissioned officers, for they have risen from the people." For years, Napoleon refused to confer the grand cross of the Legion of Honour upon Metternich and Schwarzenberg. It was only after their gallant behaviour during the fire at Schwarzenberg's mansion, that the Emperor relented, and conferred the decoration. The orders which his brother, the king of Holland, distributed with so lavish a hand, Napoleon would not allow to be worn in Paris. He sends his brother the following memorandum for kings:

"How can one give this indelible mark of appreciation to a man one does not know, to a person who may before long prove to be a rogue? Learn to know those who gather round your throne! The wish to distribute decorations should not be gratified suddenly, as one can gratify a desire to go out for a day's shooting. Noteworthy achievements must come first.

You have as yet done nothing to deserve the honour of decorating others with your effigy.

stoical than he might wish people to believe him. When Hortense's boy dies, he tells her to be composed, saying: "To live means to suffer; but the brave man is continually striving for self-mastery, and achieves it in the end."

Nevertheless, he sometimes loses his temper. The fierceness of his passion is then proportional to his pride, the irritability of his nerves, and the impatience of his creative will–the will of one who needed a thousand hands to complete his work. The stories about his threatening an ambassador with his fist, and similar outbursts of violence, are fabulous; but there is trustworthy evidence as to the terrible moment when Berthier had infuriated the First Consul by his tactlessness. Led on by Talleyrand as Mephistopheles; Berthier, in the Tuileries, had urged upon the Consul the need of assuming the title of king. Bonaparte's anger flashed from his eyes, his lips twitched, he seized the offender by the throat, and pushed him back against the wall, shouting; "Who put you up to raising my bile in this way? You will pay for it, if you dare to do anything of the kind again!"

Even amid his anger, his faculty for combination is at work, and he realises that the notion cannot have originated in the good Berthier's mind. In its psychical significance the scene is unique.

Often he is a rough, irritable soldier, who furiously lifts a badly closing window off its hinges and hurls it into the street; lashes a groom with his whip; when dictating a letter, utters curses against the addressee, which his secretary suppresses; even before the vicars-general speaks in an unseer ly way, asking. "Which of you leads this blockhead of a bishop by the nose?"

One of these vicars-general, who has been absent from duty for a long time, returns, and comes to report.

"Where have you been, misérable?"

"At home, with my people."

"How dare you stay away so long when you know that your bishop is such a damned fool?"

More important are the occasions when he simulates anger to gain some political end. Occasionally he gives the show away afterwards. "You think I was in a rage?" he says in Warsaw. "You are making a mistake. While I have been here, my wrath has never exceeded bounds." One day he is playing with his little nephew and gossiping with the court ladies, in the best of humours. The English ambassador is announced. Instantly his face changes like an actor's, his features are convulsed, he turns pale, strides towards the Englishman and storms at him for a whole hour in the presence of numerous witnesses. He is genuinely angry with England and he is genuinely annoyed at being disturbed by this visit; but the wrathful mask, the scene he makes, the angry expressions he uses, are political expedients.

The frequency of such incidents made many people believe that Napoleon was a passionate man. Talleyrand has more insight: "He's a perfect devil. He humbugs us all, even about his passions, for he knows how to act them, though they are really there!"

Self-command and coldness are so dominant in him that he never takes the vengeance that might seem appropriate to his irritable sense of honour and to the extent of his power. He never punished rivals or traitors unjustly. He only banished those whom he had good reason for wishing out of the way; and it was a point of chivalry with him to leave beaten enemies, great or small, unmolested.

Here is a scene with the Badenese envoy. The envoy asks compensation for the duke of Brunswick. The Emperor angrily refuses: not because the duke is supposed to have incited Prussia to make war against France; but because, long before this, during the first campaign against France in 1972, he had issued the famous manifesto of Coblenz, in which he had said that in Paris he would not leave one stone standing on another. "Whatever harm had this city done to him?" fiercely enquires the Emperor two decades later, the man who in those days had been Lieutenant Bonaparte. "This affront must be avenged!"

But this severity is, in the long run, out of keeping both with his own simplicity of nature and with the instincts of crowd. He could not seduce the masses by the offer of fame and money, so he showed them symbols; crowns and coronation ceremonies; courts and splendour and princes; but the people felt the growing distance between them and their ruler, and were not deceived.

When the people of Paris learned that the Emperor, in his theatre, would no longer allow King Henry to say, "I tremble," but only, "I shudder," because, though a king (being only a man) may tremble, he may not admit it–the crowd must either feel angry or become derisive. But the crowd did not hear the words in which the Emperor instructed Talma how to play Cæsar:

"When Cæsar utters his long tirade against kingship, saying, 'for me, in whom the throne inspires nothing but contempt,' he does not mean a word of what he says. He only talks like that because he knows that his Romans are standing behind him, and wishes to persuade them that the throne is an abomination to him. In reality, it is already the goal of his desire. Consequently those words ought not to be spoken with conviction."

He wants to use religion, just as he uses the drama, that he may lull the masses to sleep. Here is what the newmade Consul says to the Council of State: "What I see in religion is, not the mystery of the incarnation, but social order. It associates with heaven an idea of equality, which prevents the poor from massacring the rich. Religion has the same sort of value as vaccination. It gratifies our taste for the miraculous, and protects us from quacks; for the priests are worth more than the Cagliostros, the Kants, and all the German dreamers.... Society cannot exist without inequality of property; but this latter cannot exist without religion. One who is dying of hunger when the man next to him is feasting on dainties, can only be sustained by a belief in a higher power, and by the conviction that in another world there will be a different distribution of goods."

Through he knows all this, and though he takes kindly measures for the relief of the poor, he can never free his mind from thoughts of the rabble and the mob. When he turns from contem-

in their own), is also the source of his knowledge of men and his guide to the management of men. But always his energy interacts with other qualities. One who, for analytical purposes, would force the living whole of his character into the framework of a system, cannot avoid, from time to time, breaking threads that he may bind other threads together.

"I know not what I do, for everything depends on events. I have not a will of my own, but expect everything from their outcome.... The greater one is, the less can one have a will. One is always dependent upon events and circumstances." Such words, casually introduced into a letter from husband to wife, express the distantly visible forms of his fantasy; for only the imaginative man, not tied to systems and principles, trusts himself to the movements of the moments, allows his spirit to roam freely, and discovers his course as he goes. In this sense, his whole career is improvisation, though in the converse way from that in which most people improvise. He calculated little things in advance with great precision, whereas his world-wide designs were originated, transformed, improvised, in accordance with circumstances and developments. "One who has become familiar with affairs, despises all theories, and makes use of them only like the geometricians, not in order to move forward in a straight line, but merely to keep heading in the same direction."

This direction, this fundamental idea of the statesman, was, moreover, only possible in a man whose mind was simultaneously imaginative and mathematical. It is his most ardent vision and his coolest calculation; it is his political aim, his hope, his ambition: Europe. If this vision could be realised only by force of arms, that was because of the fierceness with which the first republic of Europe was again and again attacked by the European princes. We have seen how earnestly he strove for peace. No doubt he chose his means badly, his error being due to the time, the circumstances, and his own domineering character. But his mistakes as to method still leave undiminished the genius of the seer

appearance next day. Then the Emperor is so unhappy that he cannot eat, and pushes his plate away, saying softly and with deep melancholy: "If, in Longwood, they are going to fail in their respect for me, my lot is bitterer than if it had happened in Paris."

Gourgaud is unbearable. The young general had been through the last campaigns as Napoleon's adjutant. His affection for his chief has made him accompany the Emperor to St. Helena; but he is quite unable to overcome his feelings of wonder at his self-sacrifice. After a few weeks' sojourn on the island he meets a charming lady, and writes in his diary: "O liberty, why am I a prisoner?" He is useful to the Emperor because of his erstwhile position on the general staff; he is conversant with the science of strategy, understands maps and mathematics. Not a day goes by, however, but Gourgaud is offended. Innate vanity and jealousy are increased a thousandfold by the narrowness of the circle; he becomes the incarnation of the grotesque, which, from the first day on the island, begins to encompass the Emperor about. Gourgaud has the temperament of a snarling dog; he cannot allow Las Cases to take precedence; Napoleon vainly tries to smooth the young man's ruffled plumes, and only by resorting to command is he able to prevent a duel. "You followed me here in order to comfort my life, so you are brothers. Am I no longer here to care for you? And are you not aware that the eyes of strangers are upon you?"

The Emperor learns patience upon the rock. He also learns considerateness, especially where Gourgaud is concerned. A dozen times and more, he speaks to the young man in fatherly fashion; tries to persuade him to bear with his companions; cajoles him with the promise of a wealthy and beautiful Corsican bride. Another time he sends the general to a little festivity in the town: "You will meet the Baroness Stürmer there, and see Lady Lowe. At your age, it is always agreeable to consort with pretty women. You will go to sleep filled with pleasant thoughts, and by tomorrow morning you'll feel fit for work once more. We'll talk over the Russian campaign...." A voice from Tartarus! But the next day Gourgaud again takes offence because in a picture of the group which has been painted by one of the valets, he appears in civilian dress. A few days later he reminds his master of an episode near Brienne: Gourguad saved Napoleon's life by cutting down a Cossack who was about to attack the Emperor. The Emperor pretends to have forgotten; Gourgaud is outraged, saying that all Paris was buzzing with talk of the incident. Napoleon smiles: "You are a brave man, but amazingly childish."

Las Cases' servant steals a diamond cross belonging to Gourgaud; in order to secure peace, the Emperor has to put the cross in his own pocket, and, later, present it to Gourgaud with the assurance that he had taken it himself. Again, Gourgaud complains that he is short of money and has not enough to keep his mother in comfort. The Emperor writes: "General! We are here on a battlefield. He who runs away because he does not receive enough money, is a coward! ... I do not owe you any thanks. If you had remained in France you would have been executed, for you had a command in the '15 campaign!" In rare moments only, does the rage in his heart find such vent. Napoleon does, indeed, tell Gourgaud that he is free to leave any day he pleases. But immediately afterwards the Emperor turns the conversation on to cannons, gun-carriages, and cartridges. Next day he says:

"My dear Gourgaud, how glum you look! Have a cold rub down; that'll do you good. One must curb one's imagination, otherwise one is liable to go mad; it is like the Danube: at the source of the river one can cross it in a bound.... When I die, I shall leave no family behind me but you. I am no longer wealthy, but I have a few million still. In addition you will inherit my writings. I know what I owe you. But, while we are here, I want my friends to cheer me, and not to make me sadder by pulling long faces... Do you fancy that I have no terrible moments? At night I wake up and think of what I was and to what I have come."

When such poignant words are uttered at the table of this tiny court, all sit silent and tremble. Each one feels that from this room, this house, this island, an echo like a belated rockfall from the volcano must surely find its way to Europe's shore. For a few days thereafter, intrigues are discontinued and enmities subside. But next week, over a trifle, the quarrels break out anew. Gourgaud

never clap eyes on him once. Here is a fresh focus of intrigue and boredom. The only one of the commissioners whom the Emperor allows his suite to make friends with is Monsieur le Marquis. This is the representative chosen by His Very Christian Majesty King Louis XVIII to keep watch on his formidable predecessor. The marquis sees that Napoleon gets all the most recent periodicals; the Emperor reciprocates by the loan of books. When tidings are brought announcing the assassination in France of a Bourbon duke, General Bonaparte sends his condolences to the marquis of the old mobility by the intermediation of Count Bertrand, who is also spring of the noblesse. A scene out of comic opera!

When the prisoner is in happy vein he seeks other pastimes. One evening he spends fluttering the pages of the official year book of his reign, and says, like the bewitched tinker in the older folk-tale: "It was a fine empire. I ruled eighty-three million human beings; more than half the population of Europe!" He spends the whole of another evening with Las Cases chatting over old times. They laugh. the Emperor's spirits rise, he orders champagne to be brought, and before they realise it the hands of the clock point to eleven. Napoleon says delightedly: "How quickly the time has gone! What agreeable hours! My dear fellow, you are sending a happy man to bed."

Words which grip one perhaps more poignantly than any complaint could do.

He takes Montholon's seven-year-old child on his knee and recites La Fontaine's fable of the wolf and the lamb. The child has not fully understood, and makes a delicious muddle of lamb, wolf, and His Majesty. Another happy half hour in the Emperor's life! Again, he strolls up and down the room in the evening after dinner, humming an Italian aria, and laughing gleefully, for he has just read that King Louis always speaks of him as "Monsieur de Buonaparte." If he has a sleepless night, he makes Las Cases tell him anecdotes from the Faubourg; or he says to Gourgaud: "Let us exchange stories about love affairs, I never had enough time to spare for women. Otherwise they would have ruled my life for me." If he gets bored in his bath, he takes the opportunity of demonstrating to Gourgaud why the pressure of the water upon the floating body is equal to the weight of the body. On one occasion, in the drawing-room, he has his own height and that of his companions measured against the door.

Sometimes he will not dress or go out in the morning, putting off both until the afternoon. On one of these occasions, after an exceptionally torrid evening, he does not re-enter the house till midnight, and says that he has won a real victory by staying out so long. Another say he goes up the stair-ladder into his valet's garret, having been told that it is so nicely furnished. He is shown his own wardrobe, which is stowed away there, and is amazed to find what a lot of clothing he still possesses. He fingers the uniform he had worn as Consul (a gift from the city of Lyons), the spurs he had worn at Wagram, the cloak of the Marengo days. He makes no comment; goes down the stair-ladder in silence.

Amid these desperate attempts to kill time, does the prisoner come across no one whose situation moves him?

Yes, there is one. Of all the dwellers on this rock, the one whose lot touches the Emperor's heart most profoundly is a slave, a Malay who passes by the name Tobias, has been kidnapped, sold into slavery, and cast up on this remote island. Napoleon comes across him working in the garden, or meets him in the road, is never weary of studying him, and gives him a gold coin whenever he sees him. The Malay thanks him in broken English: "Good gentleman."

"Poor devil!" says the Emperor to his companion, obviously picturing himself in the position of this dusky piece of flotsam. "Snatched from his family, torn from his home, robbed of himself, sold into slavery! Was there ever a greater piece of wickedness? If a captain did it, he was a villain; but if the crew combined to seize poor Tobias, they were hardly responsible. Wickedness is always individual, never collective. Joseph's brethren could not make up their minds to kill him, but Judas betrayed his master."

After the next encounter with the Malay: "What a pitiful machine man, is after all! Not one bodily wrapping like another;

burden. Poor devils! Once I had been defeated, the enemy did not even bother to declare their formal deposition."

That was as far as his penitence reached. However self critical he might be, Napoleon never uttered a word of regret for having assumed a crown, or for having wished to found a dynasty. On the contrary, again and again he returned to his basic social idea: "I was the natural mediator in this struggle between the revolution and the past; my empire was in the interests of the rulers as well as in that of the peoples. My aim was the social rebirth of Europe; fate interfered before I had completed my task." In line with his general conception of kingship, he deplores that he kings should have made an end of Murat. They would have done better to show the peoples that kings are above the law. Though the guillotining of King Louis had opened the road along which he himself had advanced to a throne, he condemned the act of regicide; not because he regarded the Bourbons as competent rulers, but because continuity seemed to him essential.

For he will never misunderstand Europe's historical conditions; he will never try to establish offhand in Europe that which he dreams of establishing in the promised land of America or in the utopian island of his fancy. He always sees what is, as an outgrowth of what has been; always transforms the extant, instead of destroying it; he never wants to build entirely anew. Consequently, he does not discard the old forms, but uses them as a foundation for his new buildings. With a passion for ordering and arranging, and with a hatred for destruction, he feels how much can be done when the basis is secure. "When I rose to power, people thought I was going to be a Washington. Words cost nothing! In America, the role would have suited me well enough; there would have been no merit in adopting it on the eastern side of the Atlantic. In France, I could only become a Washington as a king among kings"

That is the truth as he sees it. Since, at bottom, he despises the purple he has hung around his own shoulders, he would have been careful to avoid taking it to America, just as Washington had resisted the solicitations of his officers. By birth, he had been neither proletarian nor prince, but a member of a petty noble family which had fallen on evil days. Thus his position was an intermediate one, sandwiched between the classes. In his conversations with Englishmen about England, he displayed the naïveté of his class fling, and his faith in the right of succession, for he closed an attack upon the British nobility in the following remarkable way:

"It is not a handful of nobles or rich men that makes a nation, but the mass of the people. True, as soon as the mob gains the upper hand it adopts an alias, and speaks of itself as the People; whereas, if it is conquered, a few poor wretches are hanged, and spoken of as robbers and rebels. 'Tis the way of the world: mob, robbers, rebels–or heroes. As the fortune of war may decide!"

After a reading of Voltaire's *La mort de César,* he remarks that in youth he had himself wanted to write a "Cæsar." One of his auditors, with a courtly double meaning, says that the Emperor has done so. Napoleon laughs the flatterer to scorn. "I? You poor babe! Yes, if I had been completely successful! But, in fact, Cæsar had no better luck than I have had–for he was assassinated!"

Closely associated with his self-criticism is his own estimate of his deeds. His historical sense, which is an integral part of his composition, leads him to an objective clarity in his contemplation of himself; perhaps an attitude of mind we may vainly seek for elsewhere in history before his day. Las Cases tells us that Napoleon talks of his career as if three hundred years lay behind him; and Countess Montholon movingly observes: "It seemed to me as if we found ourselves in another world, and I was listening to a Dialogue of the Dead."

He stubbornly defends his alleged crimes, the poisoning of the plague-stricken in Jaffa, the execution of the duke of Enghien. One day he is seized with the impulse to confide to an English physician the whole story of the Enghien episode; since, as Consul, he ran the risk of being murdered, a counterstroke was necessary. Another time he deliberately sets himself to the task of finding out what O'Meara really thinks of him. The Emperor knows the doctor to be whole-heartedly devoted to his person, but

more secure than of the great imperial treasure. Frs. 6,000,000 had been deposited in hard cash on leaving Paris in 1815.

Who are the legatees?

Montholon is to have frs. 2,000,000; Bertrand and the valet Marchand, about half a million each. The valet is the only one whom Napoleon honours with the name of friend, and he adds: "It is my wish that he should marry the widow, sister, or daughter of an officer of my old guard." Marchand, Bertrand, and Montholon are to be the executors, and all three of them have to affix their seals to each page of the will. Thus the last document penned by Napoleon's hand bears four seals; the Emperor's eagle volant, the arms of the two counts of the old noblesse, and the plain monogram of the man of the people in whom the Emperor showed supreme confidence by appointing him one of his executors. "The services he has rendered me are those of a friend."

Everyone of the servants on St. Helena receives a competence; so do the three surgeons Larrey, Percy, and Emmery. Of Larrey, Napoleon adds: "He is the most virtuous man I have ever known." Similar large sums, frs. 100,000 in most instances, are left to various generals who had been closely associated with him, to his secretaries, to two authors, the Elba guards, and the children of generals killed in battle. The stableman, the valets, the orderly officers, the huntsmen, a house-porter, a librarian, the children or grandchildren of old family friends in Corsica; the children or grandchildren of his nurse (if in need, despite previous benefactions); the children or grandchildren of his sometimes tutor in Auxonne; those of the general in command at Toulon under whom he had had his first experience of active service; those of the deputy who had helped him to get his plans put in force against Toulon; those of Muiron, "our aide-de-camp, killed at our side at Arcola, covering us with his body" –all are remembered. The next item to the Muiron bequest is a legacy. "to the subaltern officer Cantillon," who had been acquitted of the charge of attempting to assassinate Wellington. "Cantillon had as much right to assassinate that oligarch, as the latter had to send me to perish upon the rock of St. Helena. Willington, who proposed this outrage, attempted to justify himself by pleading the interest of Great Britain. Cantillon, if he had really assassinated that lord, would have excused himself, and have been justified, by the same motives, the interest of France."

This revolutionary outcry about Cantillon concludes the lists of legatees. In the instructions to the executors, the following items are enumerated: the malachite furniture from Russia: the golden table service (which was presented to him by the town of Paris); a small farm on the island of Elba which had been purchased with Pauline's money; a store of quicksilver at Venice, reckoned to be worth frs. 5,000,000; gold and jewels in a hiding-place at Malmaison; and so on, the fantastic inventory of a monarch and a adventurer.

To his mother, he leaves his silver night-lamp which has lighted many a sleepless night during his sojourn on St. Helena; each brother and sister receives a special bequest; Joseph and Lucien, as if no cloud and ever shadowed his relations with them, are mentioned calmly one after the other, each receiving "an embroidered mantle, vest, and small-clothes," though the living Napoleon had given a crown to one and offered a crown to the other.

But the principal legatee of Napoleon is his son. First of all, the boy is to have all his "arms, field-beds, saddles, spurs, snuff-boxes, orders, books, body linen, which I have been accustomed to wear and use.... It is my wish that this slight bequest may be dear to him, as recalling to him the memory of a father of whom the universe will discourse to him." Amid the inventories, which mention such items as two pairs of night-drawers and two pillow-cases, there flash out such entries as the following: "My sword, the one I wore at Austerlitz; ... my gold travelling box, the one I made use of on the morning of Ulm, of Austerlitz, of Jena, of Eylau, of Friedland, of the island of Lobau, of Borodino, and of Montmirail; ... four boxes found on the table of Louis XVIII. in the Tuileries on March 20, 1815; ... my alarm clock, it is the alarm clock of Frederick II which I took at Potsdam (in box No. III); ... a blue cloak (that which I had at Marengo); ... a consular sword; ... a

order and the problem of Europe–are valuable means of portrayal. Irrelevant was the course of the battles; irrelevant the contemporary position of the European States, in so far as this was manifested only in coalitions or antagonisms as mutable as the weather.

Every difference of opinion with his brothers or his wife, every hour of gloom or elation, his outbursts of wrath and his accesses of pallor tricks or acts of kindness towards friend or foe, every word to his generals or to women (as reported in letters or authentic conversations), seemed more important than the order of battle at Marengo, the items of the peace of Lunéville, or the details of the Continental System. What we have all learned above him at school and the university has here been restricted to a minimum; but there has been a broad demonstration of the things that are lacking amid such everyday knowledge. Yet we have not been concerned only with that Napoleon intime who is so favourite a topic with French writers; but, rather, with the Napoleonic figure as a whole, in public career and in private life, as representative of all mankind. Affairs of State and love affairs that happened on the same day, have been referred to on the same page; they derive from the same source; they determine one another; and a study of the imbroglio of the human heart will often give us more information concerning great plans than all the calculations of the tactician.

Napoleon's personality, which has no more to do with the nation for which or against which he was fighting than it has to do with morality, has not been treated here as miraculous, nor yet as split up into abstract concepts. In the episodes of his life I have tried to grasp the innermost moods (of which his rise was a natural and logical outcome), and to trace his movement towards the climax of St. Helena. To examine this man's inner life; to explain his resolves and his refraining, his deeds and his sufferings, his fancies and his calculations, as issuing from the moods of his heart–the disclosure of this *great chain of effects*, was at once the means and the end of the portrayal.

That is why there was no place in my record for portraits of the generals. Nothing could be admitted to this one volume which did not throw light upon the history of the one interior.

If we wish to give a picture of a life so full as this man's, we must perforce follow his tempo; the writer, therefore, is bound to the words of the person being described, and can never let that person speak too much. For, in truth, a man always explains himself better than anyone else can do it for him; even when he is mistaken, or when he is lying, he reveals himself to those who come afterwards, to those who know the truth. But the author must forget that he, too, knows the end. Only if, from moment to moment, he describes the feelings as they must have been experienced by one without foresight into the completed destiny, will he be able to generate that tension which, in actual life, made the sequence of events vibrant with passion.

Thus will his own sympathy, he forces the heart of the man to reveal its sympathy. In the present work, the spirit of dispassionate analysis is shown once only, towards the end. We cannot study the motor engine till it stops running.

Such a portrayal, which brings us into close proximity with its object, may give the impression of being a work of pure fancy. If, by its method of treatment, it is to be sharply differentiated from an imaginative creation, it must throughout cling to the framework of historical truth. One who believes that there is a logical succession of happenings in which there is no room for chance, will guard against retouching any detail; he will never bend a date or an incident to fit a preconceived purpose, even though, for stylistic purposes, he may think fit at times to leave one or the other unmentioned.

In this book, all the data are recorded facts, except the soliloquies. To it there might well be applied Goethe's judgment upon Bourrienne's *Memoirs:* "All the nimbus, all the illusion, with which journalists and historians and poets have surrounded Napoleon, vanishes before the awe-inspiring realism of this book: but the hero is by no means diminished thereby; he grows. We learn from this what a splendid thing truth is, when anyone has the courage to speak it." Napoleon's life is a great epic, written by the hand of fate; its full meaning will not reveal itself to one who gives

ABBREVIATIONS

Common and Self-evident abbreviations such as ch(s)—chapter(s), p—page, pp—pages, v—verse, vv—verses, Ftn—footnote, Hist. Ind. Philo—History of Indian Philosophy are not included in this list.

ABORI	*Annals of the Bhandarkar Oriental Research Institute*, Poona.
AGP	S. M. Ali's *The Geography of Purāṇas*, PPH, New Delhi, 1973.
AIHT	*Ancient Indian Historical Tradition* F. E. Pargiter, Motilal Banarsidass (MLBD), Delhi.
AP	*Agni Purāṇa*, Guru Mandal Edition (GM), Calcutta, 1957.
AV	*Atharva Veda*, Svadhyaya Mandal Aundh.
Bhā. P.	*Bhāgavata Purāṇa*, MLBD, Delhi 1973.
Bh. P.	*Bhāgavata Purāṇa*, Bhagavat Vidyapeeth, Ahmedabad.
Bm. P.	*Brahma Purāṇa*, GM. 1954.
Brn.	*Bṛhannāradiya*, Pt. Hrishikesh Shastri, Chowkhamba, 1975.
Bs. P.	*Bhaviṣya Purāṇa*, Vishnu Shastri Bapat, Wai.
Bv. P.	*Brahma Vaivarta Purāṇa*, GM, 1955-57.
CC	*Caturvarga Cintāmaṇi* by Hemādri.
DB	*Devī Bhāgavata*, GM, 1960-61.
De or GDAMI	*The Geographical Dictionary of Ancient and Mediaeval India*—N. L. De, Orienta Reprint Delhi, 1971.
Dh. S.	*Dharma Sūtra* (preceded by the author's name such as Gautama).
ERE	*Encyclopaedia of Religion and Ethics*—Hastings.
GP	*Garuḍa Purāṇa*, Ed. R. S. Bhattacharya, Chowkhamba, Varanasi, 1964.
GS	*Gṛhya Sūtra* (Preceded by the name of the author such as Āpastamba)

HD	*History of Dharma Śāstra* by P. V. Kane, G.O.S.
IA	*The Indian Antiquary.*
IHQ	*The Indian Historical Quarterly.*
KP	*Kūrma Purāṇa*, Venkateshwara Press Edt. Bombay, also Kashiraj Trust Edt., Varanasi 1971.
LP	*Liṅga Purāṇa*, GM, 1960;also MLBD, Delhi.
Mbh.	*Mahābhārata*, Gītā Press, Gorakhpur Vs. 2014.
MK	*Mārkaṇḍeya Purāṇa.*
MN	*Mahābhārata Nāmānukramaṇi*, Gītā Press, Gorakhpur VS 2016.
Mt. P.	*Matsya Purāṇa*, GM, 1954.
MW	*Monier Williams* Sk. English Dictionary, MLBD, Delhi, 1976.
NP	*Nāradiya or Nārada Purāṇa*, Venkateshwar Press, Bombay.
PCK	*Bhāratavarṣiya Prācina Caritra Kośa*, Siddheshwar Shastri, Poona, 1968.
Pd. P.	*Padma Purāṇa*, GM., 1957-59.
PE	*Puranic Encyclopaedia* by V. Mani, English, MLBD Delhi, 1975.
PJ.	*Purāṇa* (Journal of the Kashirāj Trust) Varanasi.
PR or PRHRC	*Puranic Records on Hindu Rites and Customs* R. C. Hazra, Calcutta, 1948.
ṚV	*Ṛg Veda*, Svadhyaya Mandal, Aundh
Śat. Br	*Śatapatha Brāhmaṇa.*
SEP	*Studies in Epics and Purāṇas* by A. D. Pusalkar Bharatiya Vidya Bhavan(BVB), Bombay.
SG or SGAMI	*Studies in the Geography of Ancient and Mediaeval India*—D. C. Sircar MLBD, Delhi, 1971.
SKD	*Śabda-Kalpa-Druma*—Raja R. K. Dev., Chowkhamba, Varanasi.
Sk. P.	*Skanda Purāṇa*, GM. 1960-65.

3. O Brāhmaṇa, the details of religious duties are narrated in it alongwith the accounts of various incidents, anecdotes, etc. by Pulastya to Bhīṣma with the orderly account of creation of the universe, etc.

4. The greatness of Puṣkara[1] is glorified in detail. The procedure of the Yajña of Brahman and the characteristics of the study of the Vedas (are described).

5. Various kinds of (charitable and religious) gifts and holy observances are severally glorified. The marriage of Pārvatī is mentioned. There is the long narrative of Tāraka.

6. The greatness of cows etc. that bestows all merits has been mentioned. The killing of Kālakeyas and other Daityas has been described separately.

7. O excellent Brāhmaṇa, the mode of worship of the planets and the rite of Dāna (religious gift) have been laid down. All these have been mentioned by the noble-souled Vyāsa in the first part of Sṛṣṭikhaṇḍa (Section on creation).

8. In the context of the worthiness of mother, father and others of being worshipped, there is the story of Śivaśarman[2] at first and then that of Suvrata.[3] Vṛtra's[4] death is described afterwards.

The special feature of the Pd P is that it was used by Kālidāsa for the plot of the *Śākuntala* and the *Raghuvaṁśa*. There is one special Tīrtha Māhātmya in the Pd. P. which is not mentioned by the NP and is ignored by complacent editors of the Pd. P. at Bombay (The Veṅkaṭeśvara Press edition) and Poona (The Ānandāśrama Edt.) and that is the *Karavīra Māhātmya* of 7300 verses MSS evidence of which is unanimous in claiming it to be a part of the Pd. P. It is being edited by the present editor in the Sk-Pkt. series of the Shivaji University Kolhapur.

1. As in the case of the Br. P. in the case of the Pd. P, the NP mentions only a few topics practically as tokens in each *Khaṇḍa* and passes to the next Purāṇa (Viz. the Viṣṇu)

Thus the greatness of Puṣkara mentioned in this verse (No. 4) forms Chs. 111-117 and god Brahmā's sacrifice is in Chs. 124-131 and the *Vrata* topic mentioned in the next verse (No. 5) is found in Chs. 200-258 of the Pd. P.

Hence non-mention of a topic in the NP. is not a proof that the particular topic in the Pd. P is spurious.

2. vide PD P. (Guru Mandal Edition) *Bhūmi* Khaṇḍa (Ch. 1.4)
3. ibid Ch. 11, 21, 22
4. ibid Ch. 25

9. There are the stories of Pṛthu, son of Vena[1] of Sunīthā[2] and of Sukalā.[3] There is Dharmākhyāna (narration of Virtue) afterwards.

10. There is the narrative of service rendered to the parents. There is the story of Nahuṣa. Yayāti's[4] story is narrated. Gurutīrtha[5] (Holy centre) is reviewed.

11. There is the dialogue between the king and Jaimini in which there is a very wonderful story. The story of Aśoka-Sundarī[6] is mentioned alongwith the death of Daitya Huṇḍa.

12. The narrative of Kāmoda[7] alongwith the death of Vihuṇḍa and the dialogue of Kuñjala[8] with Cyavana, the noble-souled (sage).

13. Then there is the narration of the Siddhas.[9] The benefit of (listening and recounting) this section is narrated. Then there is the dialogue between Sūta and Śaunaka. This is remembered as Bhūmikhaṇḍa.

14. The origin of the Cosmic Egg is narrated by Sauti to the sages. The situation of all the worlds including the Earth is described. Thereafter, the holy centres are enumerated.

15. Then there is the narration of the origin of Narmadā. The stories of various holy centres in it are severally mentioned. The holy account of the holy centres like Kurukṣetra etc. has been described.

16. The narration of the merit of the Kālindī, the description of the greatness of Kāśi and Gayā, and the merit-giving glory of Prayāga.

---

1. PD Chs 27-29, Vena story is scattered upto the end of *Bhūmi-Khaṇḍa.*
2. ibid Chs 33-36.
3. ibid Chs 41-60.
4. ibid Chs 64, 72-83.
5. ibid Ch. 85.
6. ibid Chs 103-116
7. ibid Ch. 119.
8. ibid Chs 86,90,122
9. ibid. Ch 123.

The above correspondence of topics in NP. verses 8-13 in this chapter and the various chapters in the Bhūmi Khaṇḍa of the Pd. P, is enough to show the nature of the *Anukramaṇikā Varṇanam* (The description of the Index or table of contents) of the Pd. P. and NP.

3. At the outset, the question of sage Mārkaṇḍeya to Jaimini is mentioned. Thereafter, the nativity of birds designated Dharma is recounted.

4. The story of their previous birth; the aberration of Divaspati (Lord of Heaven); the pilgrimage of Bala, the narrative of the sons of Draupadī.

5. The holy story of Hariścandra; the battle named Āḍībaka;[1] the narrative of the father and son (viz. Mahāmati and Sumati), then the story of Dattātreya.[2]

6. Then the story of Haihaya alongwith the great narrative, (the story of Kuvalayāśva ?) then the story of Madālasā is mentioned alongwith the story of Alarka.

7. The holy glorification of the creation is made in nine ways; the end of the period of Kalpa is pointed out, the review of the creation of the Yakṣas.

8. The creation by Rudra and others is mentioned; the activities in the continents have been mentioned; the stories of the Manus, diverse and destructive of sins, have been mentioned.

9. Among those stories, the story of Durgā is exceedingly meritorious, in the eighth Manvantara. Thereafter, the origin of Praṇava hailing from the brilliance of the three Vedas.

10. The narration of the nativity of Mārtaṇḍa alongwith its greatness; the race of Vaivasvata; then the story of Vatsaprī.

11. Then the holy story of the noble-souled Khanitra is mentioned; the story of Avikṣit and the glorification of

---

(PJ. VIII.2. (349). It is possible that when NP. was finally redacted, the stories of Rāma, Purūravas, Nahuṣa, Kṛṣṇa etc. must have been in the then MSS of Mk. P., but they came to be deleted later and the printed editions of the Mk.P. do not include them. Hence the deficiency in the number of verses.

1. The combat fought between Āḍi (an acquatic bird) and a crane into which Vasiṣṭha and Viśvāmitra had been transformed respectively due to curses given by them to each other due to the harsh treatment given by Viśvāmitra to King Hariścandra. God Brahmā intervened and stopped this duel.

2. Cf. Bh. P. I.3,52 where Dattātreya, the 6th incarnation of Viṣṇu explained *Ānvīkṣikī* to Alarka and Prahlāda.

"Kimiccha" Vrata[1] (the vowed observance called "What do you wish ?")

12. The story of Nariṣyanta, then the story of Ikṣvāku, thereafter, the story of Nala, and then the excellent story of Rāmacandra.

13. The narration of the line of Kuśa; the description of the lunar race; the holy story of Purūravas and the wonderful story of Nahuṣa.

14. The holy story of Yayāti, the enumeration of the scions of the family of Yadu; the story of infant Kṛṣṇa and then the story of his life at Mathurā.

15. The story of his life at Dvārakā, the stories of all incarnations. Then the description of the Sāṅkhya philosophy, the glorification of Sattva quality in the world.

16-18. Then the story of Mārkaṇḍeya; the benefit of listening to the Purāṇa. The man who listens to this Purāṇa called Mārkaṇḍeya with great devotion and respect, O dear one, attains the greatest goal. He who writes a gloss on this, attains the region of Śiva; He who writes the whole Purāṇa and gives it to an excellent Brāhmaṇa on the full moon day in the month of Kārttika alongwith the replica of an elephant in gold, attains the region of Brahmā. He who narrates or listens to this index (of topics in this Purāṇa) shall attain the benefit desired as in the case of the whole Mārkaṇḍeya Purāṇa.

---

1. *Kimiccha Vrata* is given in the MkP. 122.8,17,20. *Atithi* is asked what he wants and it is supplied to him. Avikṣit, the son of Karandhama carried this *vrata* of his mother and proclaimed : "O beggars (*arthinaḥ*), I have solemnly resolved to give you whatever you wish".

kimicchaiha dadāmyeṣa kriyamāṇe Kimicchike —Mk. P, 122.20

3. He has named it Skānda. There are seven khaṇḍas (parts) in it. It comprises eighty one thousand verses. It is destructive of all sins.

4. He who listens to this or reads this becomes Śiva himself. Therein all the rites and rituals regarding Maheśvara have been revealed by Ṣaṇmukha (Skanda).

5-6. These incidents which bring about all Siddhis had happened in the Tatpuruṣa Kalpa. The Māheśvara Khaṇḍa-, the first Skandha of this (Purāṇa) destroys all sins. It consists of a little less than twelve thousand verses. It is highly meritotious and contains big stories. It contains hundreds of good stories. It indicates the greatness of Skanda.

7. The following are the topics dealt with[1] in the context of the greatness of Kedāra, the Purāṇa has its starting point; thereafter the story of Dakṣa's Yajña and then the benefit of worshipping Śiva Liṅga.

Although the Veṅkaṭeśvara Edt. contains more than 12,000 verses more than the extent recorded in the NP and other Purāṇas, the Veṅkaṭeśvare edition does not include the *Mathurā* and *Māgha Māhātmyas* in the Vaiṣṇavas khaṇḍa, though the NP mentions them as a part of that *khaṇḍa*. Needless to say that the author of the NP had a different edition than those before the modern editors of the Bombay, Lucknow and Calcutta editions.

As the SK. P. is a stupendously voluminous Purāṇa a detailed analysis of all its contents is not possible here for want of space.

1. VV 7-19 mention the main topics in the Māheśvara khaṇḍa. In the GM editions it covers the following subparts, the total no. of pages of this *khaṇḍa* being 799.

Sub part.		No. of chs.	pages.
I		35	1—254
II	Kaumārikā Khaṇḍa	66	255—683
III	*Aruṇācala—Māhātmya—Pūrvārdha*	13	684—742
IV	—do— (Uttarārdha)	24	743—799

Out of the vastness of this volume, the NP. merely mentions the topics contained in the following chapters.

Section	*Chapters*
I	1-7, 9-13, 27-31, 34
II	3, 7, 8, 9, 15, 16-33, 37, 38, 39, 40, 53, 66.
III	10-11.

19. The permanent residence of Śiva in Droṇācala has ever been glorified. Thus the part of Maheśvara Khaṇḍa has been recounted.

20. The second part is called the Vaiṣṇava Khaṇḍa. Listen to the stories contained in it. At the outset, the narrative of the Earth and Varāha.

21. The greatness of the mountain Veṅkaṭa, destructive of sins is mentioned therein; the holy story of Kamalā, the residence of Śrīnivāsa therein.

22. The story of Kulāla (potter), the story of Suvarṇamukharī,[1] the wonderful tale of Bhāradvāja alongwith different narratives.

23. The dialogue between Mataṅga and Añjana that is destructive of sins, the greatness of Puruṣottama[2] (Jagannātha) in Orissa thereafter.

24. The story of Mārkeṇḍeya, the tale of king Ambarīṣa and the auspicious stories of Indradyumna and Vidyāpati.

25. O Brāhmaṇa, thereafter, there are the stories of Jāimini, Nārada and Nīlakaṇṭha, then the description of Narasiṁha.

26. The story of horse-sacrifice of the king and his attainment of Brahmaloka, the procedure regarding the Ratha Yātrā (chariot procession), the rules regarding the abode of birth.

---

*The NP. refers to the following chapters from Sk. P. II in VV 9 1-11 chs : 3-8; 9-15, 16-32, 33, 36-40, 53, 66 (from the GM edition)

The GM text of the Sk. P. devotes the whole of III—Uttarārdha to Aruṇācala.

1. VV 22-23 refer to incidents in the *Veṅkaṭācala Māhātmya* (sub-part I of this Khaṇḍa). The story of Suvarṇa Mukhari covers chs. 29-35 and the dialogue between Mataṅga and Añjana, chs. 39-40. Out of the 40 chapters of this *Māhātmya*, only the above topics are mentioned.

2. *Puruṣottama Kṣetra* is Jagannātha Purī in Orissa though originally a Buddhist shrine but before the time of the NP. it was completely Brahmanised. This *Kṣetra-Māhātmya* consists of 60 chapters which are briefly mentioned here in VV 24-28. Of special interest are *Ratha-Yātrā* (the procession of Jagannātha in a chariot) chs 33, 44. The *Śayana-Utsava* chs 43-44. NP mentions a few more stories e. g. that of Indradyumna and Vidyāpati, Guṇḍiva and Vratas like *Akāmika Pūjā*.

181. Then the stories of Sūryaprācī and Trīkṣaṇa (three-eyed) as well as that of Umānātha, the stories of Bhūddāra (the uplifter of the Earth), Śūlasthala (spot of Trident), that of Cyavana and Arkeśa.

182. The story of the holy spots of Ajapāleśa, Bālārka and Kuberasthala, the meritorious story of Ṛṣitoyā, the glorification of Saṅgaleśvara.

183. The narration of Nārada and Āditya, review of Nārāyaṇa, the greatness of Taptakuṇḍa, description of Mūlacaṇḍīśa.

184. The story of the four-faced presiding deity of the attendants and Kalambeśvara, the story of Gopālasvāmin and Vakulasvāmin, as well as the Maruts (Winds).

185. Then the stories of Kṣemārka, Unnata Vighneśa and Jalasvāmi, the stories of Kālamegha, Rukmiṇī, Durvāsā, ĪśvaraBhadra.

186. The stories of the shrines Śaṅkhāvarta, Mokṣatīrtha, Goṣpada and Acyutasadman ((Abode of Acyuta) and of the deities Jāleśvara, Huṁkāreśvara and Caṇḍīśa.

187. The wonderful story of Vighneśa stationed in Āśāpura and that of Kalākuṇḍa, the story of Kapileśa and of Jaradgavāśiva (Siva with an old cow).

188. The story of Nala and Karoṭeśvara and that of Hāṭakeśvara, the Yantra and the Bhūṣā (ornament) of Nāradeśa, Durgakūṭa and Gaṇeśa's story.

189. The story of Bhairavīs called Suparṇā, Elā and that of Bhallatīrtha, the glorification of Kardamāla and Gupta Someśvara.

190. The stories of Bahusvarṇeśa (Lord of much gold), Sṛṅgeśa and Koṭīśvara, the stories of Mārkaṇḍeśvara, Dāmodaragṛha and Koṭīśa.

191. Svarṇarekhā, Brahmakuṇḍa, the shrines of Kuntīśvara and Bhīmeśvara, the pit of Mṛgī (hind) is remembered in the temple of Sarvasva and Vastrāpatha.

192. The wonderful stories of Durgā, Bhileśa, Gaṅgeśa and Raivata, then the story of Arbudeśvara, the glorification of Acaleśvara.

193. The story of Nāgatīrtha, the description of

Vasiṣṭha's hermitage, the great eminence of Bhadrakarṇa and that of Trinetra (the three-eyed) thereafter.

194. The greatness of Kedāra, the glorification of the arrival at the holy centre, the stories of the holy centre in the form of Koṭīśvara and that of Arṣīkeśa.

195. The glorification of Siddheśa, Śukreśvara and Maṇikarṇīśa, the description of Paṅgutīrtha, Yamatīrtha and Vārāhatīrtha.

196. The greatness of Candra Prabhāsa, Piṇḍoda, Śrīmātā, Śuklatīrtha and Kātyāyanī, then the greatness of Piṇḍāraka.

197. Then the glory of Kanakhala, Cakratīrtha and Mānuṣatīrtha, the story of Kapilāgnitīrtha and that of Raktānubhandha.

198. The pilgrimage to Gaṇeśa and Pārtheśvara shrines, the story of Ujjvala, Caṇḍīsthāna (abode of the Goddess), the greatness of Śivakuṇḍa originating from Nāga, the story of Maheśa.

199. The story of Rāmeśvara and the origin of Mārkaṇḍeya, the stories severally of Uddālakeśa, Siddheśa and Gatatīrtha.

200. The origin of Śrīdevakhāta and the shrines of Vyāsatīrtha and Gautama-tīrtha, the greatness of Kulasantāra and that of the Tīrthas of Rāma and Koṭi.

201. The wonderful origin of Candrodbheda, Īśānaśṛṅga, and Brahmasthāna, the auspicious stories of Tripuṣkara, Rudrahrada and Guheśvara.

202. The greatness of Avimukta and Umā-Maheśvara, the glory of Mahaujas, the description of Jambūtīrtha.

203. The story of Gaṅgādhara and Miśraka and the eulogy of the benefit (of reading this). In the context of the greatness of Dvārakā, the story of Candraśarman.

204. The holy rite of Ekādaśī and the narration of (the mode) of worship and keeping awake (on Ekādaśī night), the description of Mahādvādaśikā and the meeting of Prahlāda and the sage.

205. The anecdote of Durvāsas, the glorification of the beginning of Yātrā (pilgrimage), the narration of the origin of Gomatī and the benefit of ablution etc., therein.

CHAPTER ONE HUNDRED AND NINE

The Brahmāṇḍa Purāṇa : Contents

God Brahmā said :

1. O dear one, listen, I shall recount to you the ancient (Purāṇa) named Brahmāṇḍa.[1] It comprises twelve thousand verses. It deals with the events of the Ādikalpa.

2. It has four Pādas (quarters), the first one is called Prakriyāpāda, then is the Anuṣaṅgapāda, the third one is Upodghāta Pāda (quarter of Introductory matter) and the fourth one is Upasaṁhāra (conclusion).

3. The first two quarters constitute the first or earlier section, the third quarter forms the middle section and the fourth quarter, the final section.

4. At the beginning, there is the stipulation of duties, then the story of the Naimiṣa forest, the origin of Hiraṇyagarbha, the conception of the different worlds.

5. This is the (summary of the) first quarter. O bestower of honour, listen to the second. The narration of the Kalpas and the Manvantaras, the knowledge of the worlds, thereafter.

---

1. According to the NP., Bh. P. (xii. 13. 8), AP. (272. 23), the Brahmāṇḍa P. consists of 12,000 verses and 12,200 according to Mt. P. 53. 54. But the Veṅkaṭeśvara edt. gives 14,286 verses. Its contents are divided into three parts (the preliminary (*Pūrva*) part containing 2 sections: *Prakriyā* (Introduction in 5 Chs.) and *Anuṣaṅga* (various *kalpas, manu-ages*, etc. in 33 Chs.) Part II (*Upodghāta*) deals with the genealogies of kings or dynastic history. Part III (*Upa-saṁhāra*) is a recapitulation of the creation of the Universe, Manu-epochs, dissolution of the Universe). It is however, called a Purāṇa with four parts (catuṣpāda) v. 29.

Kirfel in his *Purāṇa Pañcalakṣaṇa* has noted the close similarity in hundreds of verses in the *Vāyu* and *Brahmāṇḍa Purāṇas* and proposed a theory that they formed one Purāṇa originally.

The *Purāṇa* traces the tradition of authorship as follows: God Brammā→Vasiṣṭha→Parāśara→Jātūkarṇya→Vāyu or Prabhañjana→Vyāsa (vv. 33-34).

This table of contents in the NP tallies in general with those of the printed editions of the Brahmāṇḍa Purāṇa except the 40 chapters of the Lalitā episode.

(vide table of contents of the Purāṇa Edt. Jagadish Sastri MLBD, Delhi, pp ix-xi,)

6. The narration of the mental creation, the description of Rudra's offsprings, the elegance and prowess of Mahādeva and thereafter, the creation by the sages.

7. The conquest of fires, the description of the existence of Kāla (Time), the specification of the family of Priyavrata, the length and extent of the Earth.

8. The description of the (sub-continent) Bhārata and then the review of other sub-continents, the description of Jambūdvīpa and other continents, then the description of the nether-worlds.

9. The enumeration of the upper worlds, and thereafter, the movements of the planets, the narration of the Solar Array (Planetary system), the enumeration of the Divine planets.

10. The explanation of the name Nīlakaṇṭha, prowess of Mahādeva, description of the New moon day, the review of the principles of the different Yugas.

11. The institution of the Yajñas, the last two Yugas and their activity, the characteristic features of the human beings etc. in different Yugas, the description of the spiritual lineage of the sages.

12. The narration of the classification of the Vedas, the description of Svāyambhuva Manu and the enumeration of the remaining Manvantaras and then the milking of the Earth.

13. The first part, the second quarter ends with the current creation in the Cākṣuṣa Manvantara. Then in the Upodghāta quarter, the glorification of the seven sages.

14. The family of Prajāpati; the birth of the Devas and others therefrom; the desire for victory, the narration of the origin of the Maruts.

15. The narration of the descendants of Kaśyapa, the review of the families of the sages, the narration of the Pitṛ Kalpa, and thereafter, the Śrāddha Kalpa (the rituals regarding the Śrāddha).

16. The origin of Vaivasvata Manu and thereafter, the creation by him, and the family of Manu's sons, ultimately the review of the Gandharvas.

17. The narration of the family of Ikṣvāku, the family

rice grains. He should feed Brāhmaṇas with the flour of barley first fried and then ground. He himself shall partake of it.

15. O Brāhmaṇa, the man who performs the rites thus and who is devoted to Viṣṇu attains Viṣṇu's world. He is bowed to by all the Devas.

16. The third day in the bright half of the month of Jyeṣṭha is well known by the name Rambhā.[1] On that day, one should duly worship and honour an excellent Brāhmaṇa accompanied by his wife.

17-18a. With the desire for conjugal blessedness a woman should perform this holy rite and worship the Brāhmaṇa couple with scents, fragrant flowers, silken garments, etc. O Brāhmaṇa, if this holy Rambhā rite is duly observed, it yields wealth, sons, and auspicious inclination towards Dharma (virtuous and religious rites).

18b-21a. The lady who desires conjugal bliss should wear white clothes in the third day in the bright half of the month of Āṣāḍha and worship Keśava accompanied by Lakṣmī symbolised or represented in a Brāhmaṇa accompanied by his wife. She should propitiate them with meals, charitable gifts of cows, clothes and ornaments and pleasing words. By observing this Vrata, the lady shall be blessed with wealth and food-grains. By the grace of the Lord of the Devas, she shall attain Viṣṇu's world.

21b. Svarṇa-Gaurī Vrata[2] is to be performed on the third day in the bright half of the month of Śrāvaṇa.

---

1. VV 16-18 mention *Rambhā Vrata* which consists of worship of a Brāhmaṇa couple. It yields wealth, sons and inclination to Dharma. The *Rambhā Vrata* mentioned in the *Bhaviṣyottara* P. 18. 1-36 and *CC* on *Vrata* I. 426-430 is different, as it recommends that worship of Devī, and *homa*, etc. are to be performed therein.

2. VV 21b-29 describe the *Svarṇa Gaurī Vrata* to be performed by ladies, on the 3rd day of Śrāvaṇa Śu. for the propitiation of goddess Gaurī or Bhavānī. In Karnāṭaka it is observed on the 3rd day of Bhādrapada (Vrj. p. 45). Herein the number 16 is very significant. Goddess Gaurī is worshipped with 16 *upacāras* and prayed for conjugal blessedness, sons and wealth. The *Vrata* is to be observed for 16 years at the end of which a gold image of Gaurī is to be worshipped, 16 wickerworks filled with 16 edibles are to be given to 16 couples of Brāhmaṇas and the gold image to be given to the

22a-23a. The lady devotee should worship goddess Bhavānī by means of the sixteen Upacāras (articles and modes of worship and service) with the Prayer—"O goddess of holy rites, obeisance be to you. Be pleased to grant me sons and wealth, grant me conjugal blessedness. Do bestow on me all other desired things."

23b-24a. After praying thus to Bhavānī the goddess of the Devas, accompanied by God Śiva, the lady devotee, desirous of completion of the holy rite should make the gift of sweet meats etc. to Brāhmaṇas.

24b-25a. After performing this auspicious Vrata for sixteen years, she should perform the concluding ceremony of the Vrata (Udyāpana) with great devotion. She should not exhibit stinginess in the matter of expenses.

25b-28. In a pandal in a pure Maṇḍala (mystic diagram) she should perform the worship of Gaṇeśa and other gods. She should then place a flat saucer-like copper-dish over the water pot and worship a gold-image of Bhavānī therein with scents and fragrant flowers. Thereafter, the Homa should be performed. Sixteen bamboo vessels (baskets) shall be filled with sweet dishes and cooked rice, offered to the Devī as Naivedya and distributed among Brāhmaṇas, kinsmen and relatives.

29. The woman interested in the observance of this Vrata shall attain the full benefit by giving the gold image to the preceptor and monetary gifts to the other Brāhmaṇas.

30. On the third day in the bright half of the month of Bhādrapada, the lady devotee should perform the Vrata of Haritālikā[1] with great devotion, in accordance with the in-

---

preceptor. The *Vrj.* quotes a story from the *Sk. P.* about this *Vrata.* The *Udyāpana* (concluding ceremony) of this Vrata agrees with that in the Sk. P. as quoted by *Vrj.*, pp 46-47.

1. VV 30-35 describe the *Haritālikā Vrata.* This is very popular in Maharashtra but not in Gujarat or Bengal. Only women are eligible for this and they observe a fast on this day and propitiate goddess Umā and Śiva. This Vrata is found in late mediaeval digests like the *Nirṇaya Sindhu* (p. 133). *Vrj.* pp. 48 quotes the story of Haritālikā from the *Bhaviṣyottara Purāṇa.* The *Udyāpana*-rite in the NP is similar to that in the

2. The Pañcamī (fifth day) in the bright half of the month of Caitra is called Matsya jayantī. On this day, the worship of the incarnation of the Lord as (Divine) Fish is to be performed with great festivities, by devotees.

3-4a. This is called Śrīpañcamī[1] also. On this day, the worship of Śrī is to be performed by the articles of worship such as scents etc., and the Naivedyas of milk pudding etc., Lakṣmī never forsakes a person who worships Lakṣmī here (on this day).

4b-5a. Pṛthvīvrata, Cāndravrata and Hayagrīvavrata are also to be performed by those who wish to attain different Siddhis, in accordance with the respective injunctions.

5b-6a. On the Pañcamī day in the month of Vaiśākha, the man shall worship Śeṣa, endowed with the attributes of serpents. He shall attain the desired benefit.

6b-7a. The intelligent devottee shall worship the Pitṛs (Manes) on the Pañcamī day in the month of Jyeṣṭha. He shall have the acquisition of all desired benefits through feeding the Brāhmaṇas.

7b-11a. O sage, Vāyu who is present everywhere is to be worshipped on the Pañcamī day in the month of Āṣāḍha. He should go out of the village and climb up to the ridge of a mountain. To a bamboo pole he should tie a banner of five colours. It should be succintly high. He should fix the pole in the middle of the mystic diagram of a lotus. O Nārada, at its root in all the quarters, he should worship the guardians of the quarters and test the direction of the blow of the wind. Beginning with the first Yāma, (period of three hours), he shall duly worship the Lord of that quarter in which the wind blows.

---

serpents (NP. verse 61 below), though worship of Sages (*Ṛṣi-pañcamī*) in VV. 34b-48, and of goddess Lalitā (*Lalitā Pañcamī* VV. 49-53) is also given importance in the NP.

1. There are a number of days (e.g. Mārgaśīrṣa Śu. 5, Māgha Śu. 5) on which a *Śrī Pañcamī Vrata* is prescribed. The *Śrī Vrata* described in the NP. is mentioned in the *Smṛti Kaustubha* 92. VRJ. is silent about it. On this day (Caitra Śu, 5) *Vratas* called *Pṛthvī*, *Cāndra* and *Hayagrīva* are also observed.

11b. He shall thus stay there for four Yāmas without taking food.

12. He should then return home in the evening. He should partake light food. With concentration of mind and after bowing down to the guardians of the world, he should lie down on bare yet clean ground and go to sleep.

13. The dream that comes to him in the fourth Yāma (quarter) on that night shall come true. So says Śiva.

14. If anything inauspicious happens in the dream, the devotee should be engaged in the worship of Śiva and observe fast for all the eight subsequent Yāmas (i.e. 24 hours) or for the day alone (i.e. 12 hours).

15-16a. He should then feed eight Brāhmaṇas. Thereby he shall attain auspicious benefits. This holy rite is called "Śubhāśubha-Nidarśana"[1] (The test for auspicious and inauspicious results). It causes blessedness to men in this world as well as in other world.

16b. The auspicious rite called Anna-samṛddhi-da[2] (the bestower of plentitude of food) is to be observed on the Pañcamī day in the dark half of the month of Śrāvaṇa.

17-19. O Nārada, on the previous Caturthī day when there is yet some part of the day, the intelligent devotee shall put all cooked food in different vessels and pour water therein. Then he should put it in another vessel after draining off all water. The next day, after sunrise, he should worship the Pitṛs, the sages and the Devas after due ablution. He should then offer Naivedya to the Devas. With delighted mind, he shall give cooked food to beggars.

---

1. VV. 7b-16a describe a peculiar *Vrata* leading to veridical or prognosticating dreams or omens by worshipping the wind-god. No primitive Meteorology should be read in the prescription of setting up a flag on a hill-top and notice the direction of the wind per three-hour period and worship the wind-god according to its direction of blowing.

2. VV. 16b-26b deal wtth a *Vrata* giving abundance of food in every birth and aptly called *Anna-samṛddhi-Vrata* or briefly as *Anna.* The NP. prescribes this Śaiva Vrata as goddess Annapūrṇā is Pārvatī, the spouse of Śiva. Kane (HD.V. i) does not mention it. It is probably an original contribution of the NP. to *Vratas.*

This shall be worn till the end of a year. He should feed seven Brāhmaṇas with milk puddings and bid farewell to them. The intelligent devotee shall partake of it himself. In order to make Vrata perfect and complete, those fruits are given to seven Brāhmaṇas. O Brāhmaṇa, the observer of the Vrata continues it for seven years with due observances of fast. Such an observer of this Vrata attains identity with Mahādeva.

40-45a. The holy rite Śubhaśaptamī[1] is to be observed on the seventh day in the bright half of the month of Āśvina. On that day, the devotee should begin the holy rite by taking his bath and worshipping the deity. He should make excellent Brāhmaṇas read the holy books. He should then worship a Kapilā cow and pray thus—"O gentle one, I am gifting you away. May Aryamā, the sun himself be pleased. Protect you, the entire Universe, since you are born of Dharma." After praying thus, he gives the cow to a Vedic Scholar, alongwith the monetary gift. O Brāhmaṇa, after, bowing down to him, he himself should set the cow free. He should take in only Pañcagavya. Thus, the Vrata is concluded. On the next day he should feed Brāhmaṇas. He should partake of that food that is left over by them. O Brāhmaṇa, this Vrata that is performed thus, is well praised. A person endowed with faith shall attain worldly pleasures and salvation, thanks to the grace of the Lord of the Devas.

45b-47. The holy rite called Śāka Saptamī[2] is to be observed on the seventh day in the bright half of the month of Kārttika. On that day, the devotee should give seven different vegetables to seven Brāhmaṇas alongwith gold lotuses. He himself shall take in only vegetable food. On the next day, he should feed the Brāhmaṇas and give them monetary gifts as well. After bidding farewell to them, he himself should partake of the food silently alongwith his kinsmen.

48-51. The holy rite of Mitravrata is to be observed on the seventh day in the bright half of the month of Mārgaśīrṣa.

---

1. Cf. Mt. P. 79. 1-14.

2. This is a different variety of *Śāka Vrata*. For others vide HD. V, 1. P. 423.

The sun was born of Aditi and Kaśyapa and was named Mitra and Viṣṇu made him his right eye. Hence on this day, O Brāhmaṇa, the devotee shall worship him duly and feed seven Brāhmaṇas with sweets and other things. He should then bid farewell to them and take food himself. After duly performing this, the devotee shall certainly attain the world of the Sun. A Brāhmaṇa devotee attains Brahma's world and a Śūdra devotee takes his rebirth in a good family.

52-54. The holy rite called Abhaya Saptamī is to be observed on the seventh day in the bright half of the month of Pauṣa. The devotee observes fast and performs the holy rite standing on the bare ground (dharā-sthitaḥ). He worships the sun during the three Sandhyās (dawn, noon and dusk), then gifts to a Brāhmaṇa a Prastha-measure of sweet meats alongwith cooked rice soaked in milk. Thereafter, he feeds seven other Brāhmaṇas and gives Dakṣiṇā to all the eight, which may be in the form of a piece of land or gold. He then bids farewell to them and takes food himself. This is the holy rite called Abhaya. It bestows fearlessness (or Liberation from Saṁsāra) on all.

55. Other Brāhmaṇas call this by the name of Mārtaṇḍa Vrata. But learned men say that both are the same, the deity being one and the same.

56-60a. The holy Vrata called Sarvāpti[1] (Saptamī) is to be observed on the seventh day in the dark half of the month of Māgha. The devotee observes fast during the day and worships the disc of the Sun made of gold, with scents, fragrant flowers, etc. and keeps awake at night. The next day he should feed seven Brāhmaṇas with milk-puddings and give them coconuts as Dakṣiṇā. To the preceptor, he gives the gold replica of the Sun's disc alongwith other Dakṣiṇās. He should pray to him earnestly and bid farewell to him. Thereafter, he takes food himself. This is called the holy rite of Sarvāptidā. It yields all cherished desires. Thanks to the power of this Vrata, dualism (Dvaitaṁ) is achieved in every respect (? desires are fulfilled).

1. This is a special variety of this Vrata in the NP. For another variety vide HD. V. i. p. 444.

O Brāhmaṇa, the worship of the Śamī tree should be performed in the afternoon in the eastern quarter. Then, at night, in the first watch (Yāma) = 3 hours), the following (pertaining to the goddess) should be worshipped viz— sword, bow, arrows, iron club, trident, javelin, axe, dagger, leathern shield, and umbrella, banner, elephant, horse, cow and bull, book, balance, baton, noose and discus and the conch. After worshipping a buffalo with scents and other articles of worship (Upacāra), it should be chopped off and dedicated to Bhadrakālī.

21. After offering oblations and after partaking of only cooked rice, the devotee should give the monetary gifts to the Brāhmaṇa and formally conclude the Vrata.

22. He who thus worships Durgā, the destroyer of miseries and sufferings of men, enjoys excellent worldly pleasures here and shall attain heavenly region in the end.

23. The ninth day in the bright half of the month of Kārttika is glorified as Akṣaya Navamī (everlasting Navamī) On that day, the devotee should perform the rite of Tarpaṇa at the roots of Aśvattha (the holy fig tree).

24. O Nārada, with mantras special to his own branch of the Vedas, that Tarpaṇa rite of the Devas, sages and Pitṛs should be performed correctly. Then the devotee should offer Arghya to the sun.

25. Then he should feed Brāhmaṇas with sweet cooked rice. After taking his food and giving Dakṣiṇā to the Brāhmaṇas, he should rest and relax, O chief of sages.

26. It is the word (precept) of Vidhi (god Brahmā) that, if anyone performs Japa, Dāna, worship of the Brāhmaṇas, Homa thus, everything of such acts shall be entirely everlasting.

27-28a. The ninth day in the bright half of the month of Mārgaśīrṣa is glorified as Nandinī (Navamī). He who

---

Viṣṇu-dharma P. and *Vārāhī Tantra*. Kane notes more varieties and records a grant by King Pulakesin (early Cālukya dynasty) on Mahā-navamī in Kārttika (HD. V. i. pp. 373-74). In Maharashtra we worship the Śamī tree and all our implements on this day.

observes fast on that day and worships elaborately goddess Jagadambā (the mother of the Universe) with scents and other things, attains the benefit of a horse-sacrifice. There is no doubt in this respect.

28b-29a. The devotee should worship Mahāmāyā on the ninth day in the bright half of the month of Pauṣa. O Brāhmaṇa, that is conducive to the acquisition of the fruit of a Vājapeya-sacrifice provided he takes only a single meal every day.

29b-31a. The ninth day in the bright half of the month of Māgha is worshipped by the people. It is called Mahānandā as it always causes delight to men. No doubt need be entertained in this respect that the holy bath, charitable gift, Japa, Homa, observance of fast, everything performed on that day has an everlasting benefit.

31b. O excellent Brāhmaṇa, the ninth day in the bright fortnight of the month of Phālguna is of a highly meritorious nature. It is called Ānandā.[1] It is remembered as the remover of all sins. O excellent Brāhmaṇa, he who observes fast on that day and worships goddess Ānandā attains all desired benefits. It is the Truth. It is the Truth that is spoken by me.

CHAPTER ONE HUNDRED AND NINETEEN

The Holy rites to be observed on Daśami (i.e. tenth) days (in The Lunar fortnight)

Sanātana said :

1. Henceforth, I shall recount to you the holy rites to be observed on Daśamī (tenth) days (of lunar fortnights). On observing them devotedly, man becomes a favourite of Dharmarāja.

1. It appears that some *navamī Vratas* are associated with *ānandā vide Nandinī* in *Mārgaśirṣa*, *mahānandā* in *Māgha* and *Ānandā* in *Phālguna*. The last is recorded as *Ānandā* by Hemādri (*Vrata* I. 948-850). The procedure in the NP. is different from the one recorded by Kane (HD. V. i. P. 270).

pomegranate and other fruits and the plants of banana and Sṛṅgāṭaka (Trapa Bispinosa etc). After the night is over, on the next day, he takes bath and performs his daily routine. He should then worship Gadādāmodara with all the sixteen Upacāras and with the recital of the Puruṣasūkta. After feeding Brāhmaṇas and giving them Dakṣiṇās to their satisfaction, he should bid farewell to them. He shall give that gold image to the preceptor alongwith a cow. He who respectfully performs this Bodhinī Vrata with devotion, enjoys all worldly pleasures and attains the region of Viṣṇu.

56b-59a. On the eleventh day in the dark half of the month of Mārgaśīrṣa, the devotee observes fast of Utpannā (or Utpatti) Ekādaśī. On the Dvādaśī day, he should worship Lord Kṛṣṇa with scents and other requisites of services or upacāras. He then feeds leading Brāhmaṇas and gives them Dakṣiṇas. After bidding them farewell, he should take food himself alongwith friends and kinsmen. He who performs the Utpannā (or Utpatti) Ekādaśī Vrata with devotion, rides an aerial chariot and attains the region of Viṣṇu.

59b-62a. On the eleventh day in the bright half of the month of Mārgaśīrṣa, the devotee observes the holy rite of Mokṣā (Mokṣadā) Ekādaśī by fasting. On the Dvādaśī day, in the morning, he worships Ananta who is the embodiment of the Universe, with all the Upacāras. The Brāhmaṇa devotee then feeds the Brāhmaṇas. He bids farewell to them after giving them Dakṣiṇā. He then takes food alongwith the kinsmen. O Brāhmaṇa, by performing this Vrata, he enjoys all the desired worldly pleasures. He uplifts ten generations of his ancestors and ten generations of successors. He then attains Hari.

62b-64a. On the eleventh day in the dark half of the month of Pauṣa, the devotee observes the holy Saphalā Ekādaśi rite. On the Dvādaśī day, he worships Acyuta with all Upacāras. After feeding Brāhmaṇas with sweet-meats and giving them Dakṣiṇās, he bids them farewell. O Brāhmaṇa, after performing the Saphalā Ekādaśī Vrata thus in accordance with the injunctions, he enjoys all worldly pleasures here (in this world). In the end, he goes to the region of Viṣṇu.

64b-67a. On the eleventh day in the bright half of the month of Pauṣa, the devotee observes the holy rite of Putradā

Ekādaśī. On the Dvādaśī day, he should worship the discus-armed Lord with Arghya and other Upacāras. Thereafter, he should feed leading Brāhmaṇas. After giving them Dakṣiṇā, he should bid farewell to them and eat the cooked rice left over, alongwith his loving kinsmen. O Brāhmaṇa, he who performs the holy rite thus, enjoys all desired pleasures, in the end; he rides in an aerial car and goes to Hari's abode (Vaikuṇṭha).

67b-70. On the eleventh day in the dark half of the month of Māgha, the devotee observes the holy rite of Ṣaṭtilā Ekādaśī. He takes bath with gingelly seeds; he makes gift of them; he uses them in the Tarpaṇa rite; he performs Homa with them; he eats them and he worships with them on the morning of the Dvādaśī day. After perfectly worshipping Vaikuṇṭha (Viṣṇu) with all the Upacāras, he feeds the Brāhmaṇas. Then he bids farewell to them, after Dakṣiṇā has been duly paid, O Brāhmaṇa, by performing the holy rite, thus in accordance with the injunctions, the devotee, with great concentration, enjoys all desired pleasures here. In the end he attains Viṣṇu's region.

71-73. On the eleventh day in the bright half of the month of Māgha, the devotee observes the holy rite of Jayā Ekādaśī. On the day of Hari, in the morning, O Brāhmaṇa, he should worship Puruṣa, the Lord of Śrī. After feeding, giving Dakṣiṇā and bidding farewell to the Brāhmaṇas, he should take in the food left over by them alongwith his kinsmen. He should be pure, in mind and body. O Brāhmaṇa, he who thus performs the holy rite that propitiates Keśava, enjoys excellent pleasures here. In the end, he shall attain the region of Viṣṇu.

74-76. On the eleventh day in the dark half of the month of Phālguna, the devotee observes the holy rite of Vijayā Ekādaśī. On the Dvādaśī day, in the morning, he worships Yogīśa (the Lord of Yogins) with scents and other things. He feeds Brāhmaṇas and gives them Dakṣiṇās to their satisfaction. After bidding them farewell he should himself silently take food in the company of his kinsmen. The man who performs the holy rite thus, enjoys the desired pleasures. After death, he goes to Viṣṇu's region. He is well honoured by the Devas.

opportunity to take bath in the Gaṅgā, it is more efficacious than a crore such baths at the juncture of solar eclipses.

15. This is an auspicious combination in regard to the worship of Kāma, viz : the constellation of Śatabhiṣak, Saturday and the bright half of the month of Caitra. It is famous by the name of Mahāmahā.[1] It yields salvation to a crore of the members of his family.

16-18a. On the thirteenth day in the bright half of the month of Vaiśākha, the holy rite of Kāmadevavrata is to be observed. The devotee should observe fast and worship Kāma with scents etc. Thereafter, every month, on the thirteenth day in the bright halves, he should perform the holy rite in the same manner. At the end of the year, in order to achieve the Sāṅgatva (the status of having the complete fulfilment of the Vrata) of the holy rite, he should give a cow bedecked with ornaments to a Brāhmaṇa after duly honouring him.

18b-22a. The holy rite of a Daurbhāgya-Śamana-Vrata[2] (i.e. the holy rite for quelling misfortunes) is to be observed on the thirteenth day in the bright half of the month of Jyeṣṭha. The devotee should take the holy dip in the river water and worship the following three plants growing in clean spots : the white Mandāra, the white Arka, (the sun-plant) and the red Karavīra (the oleander). Gazing at the sun in the sky, he should utter this mantra and pray : "O Mandāra, O Arka, O Karavīra, you are all born in the family of the sun. Worshipped by me, quell my misfortune; obeisance be to you all." If any one devotedly worships the three plants thus every year, his misfortune is quelled. No doubt need be entertained in this regard.

22b-28a. On the thirteenth day in the bright half of the month of Āṣāḍha, the devotee should take in only one meal a day. According to his ability, he should get the image of Umā

---

1. The complete name of the *Vrata* is *Mahāmahā Vāruṇī vide* HD. V. i. 405-406.

2. This *Vrata* shows how the cult of 'tree-worship' of Pre-Aryans in India was observed in Hinduism. A number of trees e.g. The Pippala (Aśvattha), Vaṭa Bilva, Tulasī-Aśoka (*vide* VV. 41-45 below) and others have been firmly established as 'deities' in Puranic Hinduism.

and Maheśvara made in gold, silver or clay. The goddess and the Lord of the universe are represented as seated respectively on a lion and on a bull. O Nārada, the images are installed and consecrated in a temple or in a cowpen or in the house of a Brāhmaṇa, by the divine Mantras. Then the worship is continued for five days and the Vrata (vow) of taking a single meal is kept up. On the Tṛtīyā (third) day, the devotee takes his bath in the morning and worships the deities once again. The images are to be given to a Brāhmaṇa who is a master of the Vedas and the Vedāṅgas (ancillaries of Vedas). This Vrata is continued from year to year for full five years. At its end, he should give those images (to a Brāhmaṇa) alongwith a pair of cows, If the devotee, whether a man or a woman, performs this auspicious Vrata thus, he never experiences a break in the conjugal love in the course of seven births.

28b-32. The auspicious, holy rite of Ratikāma-vrata is to be observed on the thirteenth day in the bright half of the month of Śrāvaṇa. It prevents widowhood of ladies. It is conducive to the increase in the number of children, O excellent Brāhmaṇa, the virgin or the woman devotee observes fast. The images of Rati and Kāma are made of copper, clay, gold or silver and placed in a similar vessel. She should then properly (according to injunctions) worship them with scents etc. Then she invites a Brāhmaṇa couple for the following Caturdaśī day. After honouring them and feeding them, she should give them images alongwith monetary gifts. This excellent Vrata is continued for fourteen years. For completing the Vrata, the images are to be given along with a pair of cows.

33-40. The holy rite of go-tri-rātra[1] is to be observed on the thirteenth day in the bright half of the month of Bhādrapada. The image of Lakṣmīnārāyaṇa is made of gold or silver. On an auspicious Maṇḍala (mystic diagram) of a lotus of eight petals, the image is to be placed on a pedestal covered with a

1. Kane records three varieties of *Go-tri-rātra Vrata* out of which this is the second and is described by Hemādri (*Vrata* II. 293-303). It is a synthesis of Viṣṇu-worship and cow-worship.

observes fast and pours nectar like water at the root of the Vaṭa (Banyan tree).

10. She should encircle with threads the holy tree and circumambulate it one hundred and eight times. Thereafter, she should pray to the divine and highly chaste lady Sāvitrī :

11. "O Mother Sāvitrī, who considered your husband a deity, you are the mother of the Universe. You are worthy of being worshipped by the whole universe. O gentle lady present in this Vaṭa tree, obeisance to you. Grant me nonseparation from my husband.

12. After praying thus she goes home. On the next day, she shall feed Suvāsinīs (married women whose husbands are alive) and take food herself. She shall be blessed with conjugal bliss.

13-15. The holy rite of Go-padma[1] is prescribed for performance on the full moon day in the month of Āṣāḍha. After taking his bath the devotee meditates on Hari thus :

"He has four arms and a huge body. He has the lustre of gold. He appears beautiful with the conch, discus, iron

---

circumambulating the tree one hundred and eight times and weaving a thread round it all the while, prayer of Sāvitri (associated with the tree) for sparing oneself from widowhood and feeding *Suvāsinis* the next day after which the lady observer of the Vrata breaks the fast.

This Vrata is observed on Jyeṣṭha Kṛ. 30 also (infra verse 85). The story of Sāvitri who brought back her husband from the god of death is extremely popular (vide *Mbh.-Vana* Chs. 293-299, Mt. P. Chs. 208-214 the *SK. P.-Prabhāsa* Ch. 166). The *Vrata* consists of fast for three nights which the NP. fails to prescribe. Its mention in the AP. 194. 5-8 shows that the *Vrata* was in vogue before the 10th Cent. A.D. It is said that the *Vrata* is called *Vaṭa-Sāvitrī* as it was under the shade of a *Vaṭa* tree that Satyavān (Sāvitrī's husband) went and took hold of its branch before he collapsed.

The banyan tree with its spreading branches symbolises the spread of one's race. Perhaps pre-Aryans worshipped this tree for increase and spread of their race and the story of Sāvitrī came to be associated with it while it was being Brahminised.

1. VV. 13-17 describe the *Go-Padma Vrata*. The NP. fails to justify the title *Go-Padma* of this Viṣṇu Vrata. The girl or woman has to draw 33 figures of cows foot-print everyday during the *Vrata*. Hence its title *Gopadma*. For details vide VRJ., pp. 301-302.

club, lotus, goddess Lakṣmī and Garuḍa. He is served by sages, Devas, Yakṣas, Gandharvas and Kinnaras."

(After meditation) he should worship the Lord by means of the Puruṣa Sūkta, and with scents and other Upacāras.

16 He should propitiate the preceptor with clothes, ornaments and other things as well as with affectionate mind. He should feed Brāhmaṇas and others with sweet cooked rice according to his capacity.

17. O Brāhmaṇa, by performing this Vrata, the devotee undoubtedly, derives his cherished desires both here and hereafter, thanks to the grace of the Lord of (Kamalā) Lakṣmī.

18-21. The holy rite of Kokilā Vrata is to be observed on this very same day. The rules of procedure are now described. The observance is from this full moon to the next full moon in the month of Śrāvaṇa. The woman should take her bath in the water outside the house (i.e. in a river or a tank). She should meditate on goddess Pārvatī as follows : "Gaurī has the form of a cuckoo with golden wings, jewelled eyes, louts-like face, having the lustre of coral and the complextion of musk. She is born in the heavenly Nandana Park, seated on mango and Campaka trees cooking out exquisite song." Her figure is painted in colours on cloth. The devotee worships her every day with scents and other things.

22. O Brāhmaṇa, when the Vrata is concluded, she devoutly should give a Brāhmaṇa the image of the goddess in gold or ground flour of gingelly seeds, alongwith a gold piece as Dakṣiṇā. The following Mantra is uttered.

23. "O Goddess Kokilā, born in the park of Citraratha, O beloved wife of Hara, you have been worshipped and given to a Brāhmaṇa. Be the cause of happiness to me."

24. He should then feed the Brāhmaṇa and thirty Sanyāsinīs if possible, otherwise one, and give clothes etc. and Dakṣiṇā in accordance with her capacity. After bowing to them she should bid farewell to them.

25. O Nārada, the woman who performs this excellent Kokilāvrata attains happiness and conjugal bliss in the course of seven births.

26-28. On the full moon day in the month of Śrāvaṇa is

4. O sage, born of the four-faced deity (Brahmā), there is nothing that is unknown to you in the three worlds. O prominent Brāhmaṇa, the three - fold things (of the past, present and future time) are precisely known to you.

5. The sin committed unknowingly is called Śuṣka (dry) and the sin committed knowingly is cited as Ārdra (wet). Please tell us the three events: that which are yet to be (future), that which has passed by (past), and that which is current (present).

6a. What is that fire whereby the sin may be reduced to ashes? This is esteemed by me (i.e. what I want to know).

Vasiṣṭha said :

6b-9. O mighty king, may it be heard what that fire is whereby it is possible to reduce to ashes completely the dry as well as the wet kinds of sin. A person who, on the day of Lord Viṣṇu (i.e. Ekādaśī day) with due control of sense-organs observes fast, worships the killer of demon Madhu (i.e. God Viṣṇu), takes bath in water containing Emblic Myrobalan and keeps awake during that (Ekādaśī) night, completely absolves himself of all sins like a gambler losing all his wealth.

10. O king of kings, the fuel of sins even though accumulated (lit. generated) in the course of hundred births, is reduced to ashes through the fire called Ekādaśī.

11. O king, there is nothing that sanctifies men so much as the day of Padmanābha (i.e. Ekādaśī) that destroys sins.

12. O ruler of men, sins remain in this body, only so long as the creature (i.e. man) does not observe fast on the auspicious day of Padmanābha.

---

arose, god Indra came forward and said, "He will suck me" (*māṁdhātā*). The Pd. P. tells us that when there was a drought for the continuous three years, the sages advised him to observe Ekādaśī Padma-nābhā (i.e. Padmā). He observed Ekādaśī Vrata and made all his subjects to follow it. Rains showered, people became happy and the king prospered (Pd. P. VI—*Uttara Khaṇḍa*, Ch. 58. 33-38.

A proper setting for glorifying the *Ekādaśī Vrata* with Māndhātā as an interlocutor. But it is after two benedictory verses that Māndhātā is *abruptly* introduced. In fact no background is provided to this dialogue between Māndhātā and Vasiṣṭha, his family priest.

13. Thousands of horse-sacrifices and hundreds of Rājasūya sacrifices do not deserve even a sixteenth part of the fast observed on the Ekādaśī day.

14. O Lord, all the sins that have been committed by the eleven sense organs shall be dissolved, thanks to the fast on the Ekādaśī (eleventh) day.

15. O king, there is nothing equal to Ekādaśī that is destructive of sins. Even if it is observed under a pretext it exempts one from seeing the son of the Sun-god (i.e. Yama, the god of death and Hell).

16. It bestows heavently pleasure and salvation; it yields kingdom and sons; it grants good wives and freedom from ailments to the body.

17-18. O king, neither Gaṅgā, nor Kāśī, nor Gayā, nor Puṣkara, nor Kurukṣetra nor the river Revā, or the Devikā,[1] and neither the Yamunā nor the Candrabhāgā are more meritorious than the day of Hari. O leading king, Hari's abode is attained without any strain.

19. By observing fast during the day on the day of Hari and by keeping awake during the night, a man is liberated from sins and he goes direct to the region of Viṣṇu.

20. O leading king, it uplifts ten generations on the mother-side, ten generations on the father's side, and ten generations on the wife's side.

21-23. O Sovereign king, he leads his own soul to the city of Viṣṇu. This rite of fast is like the Cintāmaṇi (wish-yielding stone) or it is equal to a Nidhi (treasuretrove) or it is like the Saṁkalpapādapa (wish-yielding tree). O the most excellent one among kings, those who resort to Dvādaśī (i.e. after observing fast on the previous day who break fast on this day) put forth two more arms (become like viṣṇu four-armed), they ride on the enemy of serpents (i.e. Garuḍa) as their vehicle, they will be having garlands and yellow garments (like Viṣṇu). Thus they go to Hari's abode.

---

1. The southern portion of the river Sarayū—De. p. 55. According to *Kālikā* P., (Ch. 53), Devikā is a distinct river between Gomatī and Sarayū and joins at the confluence of Gaṇḍak and Gaṅgā and the confluence is called Triveṇī.

thereof. But O Brahmā, the seed that originates from the nurse is sown by another. It may perhaps redeem both the sides, the one who is offered the Piṇḍa and the one to whom the body belongs. But the wife has no seed nor the wife holds him in her womb. Then, O Lord of the Universe, how does her side attain the greatest region through the greatness of the merit of the son-in-law ? Therefore, my head aches.

20. O Lord, no purpose of mine is served, thanks to this sort of employment, whoever observes fast on the Ekādaśī day leaves me off and goes to Hari.

21. O Lotus-born deity, he uplifts three generations including himself. After leaving off my path, he goes to Hari's mansion.

22-24. No man attains such a destination as that of a devotee who performs the holy rite of Viṣṇu—Not even if he performs sacrifices (Yajñas), goes on pilgrimage to the holy centres or gives charitable gifts or performs those Vratas with the exception of those pertaining to Viṣṇu. No one giving up life in water or fire attains such a goal. O god Brahmā neither the person who gives up his body by the Yoga practice nor he who falls down from a precipice attains that goal. O most excellent one among those who attain good goals, it is the truth that has been uttered by me.

25. Any human being, even if he perpetrates extremely wicked actions, goes to the world of Dharaṇīdhara (Viṣṇu who holds and supports the Earth). If the man smears his limbs with the fruits of embylic myrobalan and if he has no interest in sweet juices and meals on the Ekādaśī day.

26. I have become disappointed because I have no work on the Earth. Hence, I have resorted to your pair of lotuslike feet. O cause of creation, sustenance and dissolution (of the universe) make time propitious for the attainment of fearlessness on this mere intimation.*

*But if the reading is *sarga-sthiti-nāśa-hetoḥ* as in my text, the verse means.

"O Lord, who grant immunity from fear by mere request, fix up the time for attaining creation, sustenance and destruction."

27. May not the sinful men be devoid of restraint through my Bhūtagaṇas (attendants). Let them be chained or tied with ropes. Let them come near me and be under my control.

28. The path oppressed by the heat of the sun is broken because crowds of people are being released very quickly at the hands of Viṣṇu's attendants from the hell Kumbhī. They go to the splendid abode of the lord who is greater than the greatest.

CHAPTER FIVE

The lamentation of Yama

Yama continued:

1. The path of the discus-bearing lord has been furnished and rubbed, O deity worshipped by the three worlds, by men who pass through it without break.

2. O Lord of the Universe, I consider the world of Viṣṇu to be infinite in magnitude, since it is not filled with the floods of people with all living beings cropping up like lotuses.

3-4. O Pitāmaha, (Grandsire of the universe) people adhering to their duties, people following other men's duties, pure people and impure people, every one observes fast on the day of Viṣṇu and goes to the world of Viṣṇu, at the behest of the king. The entire world is accommodated only in the residence of Mādhava. This king is hence our great enemy. He is particularly your enemy as well.

5. O Lord of the worlds, undoubtedly he must be curbed and restrained. For the last one thousand years, he has ruled over the sphere of the world.

6-8a. Immeasurable number of persons have been taken over by him to the world beloved of Hari. They were enabled to ride Garuḍa. They were given forms having four arms; they were neatly clad in yellow garments; they were garlanded and smeared with sweet-smelling unguents. If he

in the activity of protection (i.e. abiding by my duty as their protector) I have never enjoyed or slept of my own accord.

12. O son, As long as you were unable to shoulder the responsibilities of the kingdom, ease and happiness was not attained by me, as I was determined to restrain those who partook of food on the day of Lord Viṣṇu (i.e. on Ekādaśī days).

13. Among the people some (i.e. Śaivites) followed the path of the devotees of Śiva. Some abided by the path of the Sun, others were the followers of Brahmā, while others (i.e. Śāktas) stood in the path of Pārvatī.[1]

14-16. (Many excuses were offered by people for eating food on Ekādaśī day). "In the morning and in the evening, we are sitting up and performing the Agnihotra (Fire-worship) rites. Moreover a small boy, a young man, an old man, a pregnant woman, a small girl, a sick man or a physically handicapped person cannot undertake a fast." When people protested like this, I refuted them everywhere by means of words mentioned in the Purāṇas. I spent many days over this. For the purpose of abiding happiness of the subjects, I enlightened them in various ways.

17-18. I chastised them and made them desist from taking food. The scholars were made to refrain from food (on the authority of sacred scriptures (i.e. they were convinced that sacred texts prescribed the Ekādaśī rite). The ignorant people were made to refrain from taking food by chastising them by means of deterrent punishment. Thus all were forced to observe fast on the day of Hari. Thereby being thus engaged I did not enjoy any personal happiness on the Earth.

19. O dear son, the king who wishes to protect his subjects shall not inflict on them miseries from himself or from others (from his own people or officers or through enemies).

---

1. This shows that at the time of the NP, the sects of god Brahmā and Sun were equally prominent like the Vaiṣṇava, Śaiva and Śākta sects.

20. To such a king ever-lasting worlds have been declared (as a reward) in the Purāṇas. I exist for the sake of the subject O gentle boy, and never for myself.

21. I wish to enjoy the pleasures derived from hunting and other strenuous exercises. O son, I never desire the pleasures of drinking bouts and gambling.

22-23. Dear son, a king indulging in these vices will perish ere long. Through your favour, my dear son, I wish now to roam about the mountains, forests, rivers and lakes of diverse kinds under the pretext of hunting. After entrusting you with the burden of kingdom, I am desirous of enjoying covetable pleasures.

24. All these things which I had in my mind have been disclosed to you. If they are carried out, you will earn a great fame; if they are not done, you will fall into hell.

Dharmāṅgada said :

25. "I shall do all these things. Enjoy the pleasures that appeal to your mind. O dear father, I shall bear the heavy burden of kingdom with pleasure.

26. No other holy virtue except the execution of your behest is acceptable to me. A son who does not act according to the directives of his father incurs fall, though he may be performing holy rites.

27. Hence, I shall carry out your order : Here have I joined my palms (in reverential promise)." When these words were spoken, the king became delighted.

28. Learning again the availability of the game, Rukmāṅgada became desirous of going to the forest. Dharmāṅgada was delighted in his mind. He summoned his subjects and said :

29. "I have been commanded by my father to strive for your protection and welfare. My father's behests must be carried out in every respect by me who wish for the attainment of Dharma.

30. O subjects, a son has no other Dharma (holy duty) except the execution of the directives of his father. When I hold the rod of justice, even Yama cannot be the chastiser.

8. O Mohinī of charming limbs, for a contact with you I will give even my soul; what then about wealth, gems etc? Be favourable to me.

9. On hearing the words of the king Mohinī smiled, raised the king up and said in sweet voice.

10. O king, I do not wish to choose the Earth alongwith the mountains and oceans.. Whatever I say on a certain occasion must be carried out without hesitation.

11-12. I will resort to you. There is no doubt about it. Enter into this agreement with me.

The king said :

O gentle lady, I will enter into that agreement whereby you shall be satisfied. For want of the sexual contact with you my body has attained well nigh the tenth state (of a loveborn person).

Mohini said :

13. Give unto me your right hand that has practised many holy rites, whereby I will be able to believe in your words, O king.

14. You are a king. You practise religious and holy rites regularly. You have won fame for truthfulness in the three worlds. You will never utter a lie on any occasion. Still this is a worldly convention of making you promise which has been followed by you.

15. When Mohinī said these words, the king who was overwhelmed with mental agony said with a delighted heart.

16. O beautiful lady, I have never uttered a lie since my birth. O fair-complexioned lady, even in the course of fun and sports I have never spoken a lie.

17. Or of what avail are these words uttered by me by way of convincing you in so many words? Look that my right hand, marked by merits, is offered to you.

18. O beautiful woman, of lovely thighs, if I do not carry out your words, whatever merit has been accumulated by me ever since my birth shall become yours.

19. (In case I fail to carry out your words) my virtue and piety have been given in exchange to you. O lady become my wife. I have been forcibly and extremely perturbed and excited by your beauty.

20. I am a king by name Rukmāṅgada, the son of Ṛtadhvaja, born in the race of Ikṣvāku. Dharmāṅgada is my son.

21. O lady of charming eyes, under the pretext of hunting the deer, I have entered the forest. Then the pleasant hermitage of Vāmadeva was seen by me.

22. Something was mentioned by that sage. Thereafter I was bid adieu by him. Riding on my excellent horse I came here to see mount Mandara.

23. With my mind curious and enthusiastic I was roaming over the excellent mountain, when the sweet song emanating from your mouth reached my ears.

24. Attracted by that song, I have approached you. O lady of charming eyes, you have come within the range of my vision.

25. Thereafter, O gentle lady, I fell unconscious on the ground. Now I have regained consciousness, thanks to your nectarine words.

26. O enchantress of the worlds, I consider myself as a person born again. It behoves you to favour me by replying to me suitably.

27. On being requested by the king thus, Mohinī spoke in reply :—

O king, I am born of God Brahmā and have come here for your sake.

28. On hearing about your fame, I was overwhelmed by Cupid. I have forsaken all gods, the chief of whom was Indra, and come to the golden mountain of Mandara.

29. With my mind in concentration, I stayed here engaged in penance. I am worshipping God Śaṅkara, the Lord of the Devas, by offering (singing) songs unto him.

30. I consider presentation of music is the great favourite of the deities. O king, it is superior to all other Dānas (charitable gifts) and it is the bestower of endless salvation.

CHAPTER SIXTEEN

The Anecdote of a chasle Lady

Vasiṣṭha said :

1. On hearing the words of Dharmāṅgada, Rukmāṅgada became delighted and said : It is true, O son, your new mother has been obtained by me on the Mandara mountain.

2. She is the daughter of Vedāśraya (support of the Vedas i.e. Brahmā). Formerly, O dear son, she had been performing a terrible penance on the divine mountain Mandara, with the determination of attaining me.

3. Some fifteen days before I started from here, riding on the horse I reached the Mandara, the most excellent of the mountains, containing many metals and minerals.

4. This damsel of comely appearance was seen by me seated on the top of the mountain, propitiating Maheśvara and engaged in singing.

5. Hit by the arrows of Anaṅga (the God of Love), I became unconscious and fell on the ground like the deer hit by a hunter.

6. Thereafter, I had been shaken (and revived into) consciousness)by this gentle lady of charming eyes; with some importunity I have been chosen as her husband.

7. I too have taken the pledge with offering of my right hand. This lady of large eyes has been made my wife by me on the top of the mountain.

8. Descending to the ground level (at that foot of the mountain), we got up on to the horse. Hurried (travelling therefrom) we have come to you within three days.

9.-11. On my way I had the pleasure of seeing mountains, different lands, lakes and rivers. O son, she is your mother. She would heighten your pleasure. Make obeisance to this lady of charming limbs as though to your own natural mother. On hearing the words of his father, the son, the suppressor of his enemies, bent down his head as far as the ground level and spoke these words :— O gentle lady, O dear mother, favour me. I am your son, servant and slave.

behest of my father, I shall render personal service unto her. On saying this he entered the mansion and grasped the hands of his step-mother. After walking fifteen steps, they reached the cot. He made Mohinī sit there.

28-29. It was made of gold with silk cloth spread over. It was soft and firm. A soft bed-sheet was spread over it. It was bedecked in gems and jewels. Many jewelled lamps having the refulgence of the sun, were fitted on to it. Thereafter, the prince who had virtue as his ornament (i.e. Dharmāṅgada) offered water for washing the feet of Mohinī.

30-31. The prince considered her even elderly to Sandhyāvalī. His mind did not have any ignoble feelings towards Mohinī. Though he was beautiful and graceful and she a charming lady with plump and stout thighs, buttocks and breasts, he considered her a lady ten thousand years old and himself a boy of three years.

32. After washing her feet, he applied (sprinkled) that water on his head. With the head bent down in humility he said : Mother, I am meritorious (with you as my mother).

33. After saying this, he dispelled her fatigue by his own efforts and by those of men and women (servants). With great joy he placed all means of pleasures at her disposal.

34-35a. At the time of the churning of the milk ocean two earrings were produced. They used to emit nectarine juice. These were acquired by Dharmamurti.[1] After conquering Dānavas in the Pātāla (nether worlds). Vṛṣāṅgada (i.e. Dharmāṅgada) himself put these in the ears of Mohinī.

35b-36a. A necklace of a thousand and eight auspicious white pearls each like the fruit of the embylic myrobalan was put on the bosom of the gentle lady.

36b-37. Then the prince offered her a subsidiary light necklace of gold coins of a hundred Palas inset with ten thousand diamonds to his mothers. He gave her twice eight

---

1. VV. 34-46 contain reference to the history of some rare ornaments acquired by Dharmāṅgada and gifted to Mohinī. I could not trace it in other purāṇas.

54. On hearing the statement of the son, all of them were thrilled with delight..They spoke to their husband the king. "Sport with the daughter of the self-born deity for a long time like the leading scion of the family of Raghu, (Rāma) with the daughter of the king of Videha (i.e. Sītā).

55. There is no doubt about it that the daughter of Brahmā cannot be a cause of poignant grief to us because of her sexual connection with you. Know that these words are uttered by us without any heart-burning misery. Thanks to the brilliance of your son.

CHAPTER NINETEEN

The love-making of Mohini

Vasiṣṭha continued:

1. The king who was passionately fond of his lady-love, on being permitted by his wives, derived incomparable delight. He spoke to Dharmāṅgada thus :—

2. "O son, protect this Earth consisting of seven island-continents after slaying the wicked at the outset. Be ever vigilant and alert and active.

3. Always make use of the best opportunites. Be a supervisor of good conduct. Be always conscious of everything and alert, be favourable to good business transactions.

4. Be moving continuously; always be interested in charitable gifts; always eschew crookedness, be always engaged in the disciplined life of the good.

5. O son, listen to another thing which should be pursued by you now. Lack of trust and confidence in everything and everyone is recommended in the case of kings.

6. O popularly loved one, (you must possess) the accurate knowledge of the treasure and of the (assets of the) people.

You should elicit money (taxation) like the (absorption of) flowery juice by a bee gathering honey (from flowers).

7. Through you as my son, I feel that youth has been regained by me.

8. After delightfully entrusting you with the burden of the earth with its seven oceans and continents and having obtained this moon-faced wife of excellent and rare beauty and seductive charms, I shall enjoy myself in dalliance.

9. In the human world, a father overcome with wrinkles, shaking old teeth and white greying hairs becomes a cause of shame and (derisive laughter) if he is desirous of sexual intercourse, when the son has attained muturity and is competent.

10. Though aged, I am not weak and infirm; I am flourishing in happiness, I desire this fair lady the most beautiful in the world, who for my sake has forsaken even the Devas; this lady of sweet and charming eyes, who has been smitten by the arrows of Cupid, has come to me (of her own accord).

11. I will engage myself at will in sexual dalliance with this lady of the lustre of molten gold, my mind shall then be full (thanks to the realisation of my cherished desires). After hiding myself on the banks of rivers of divine beauty as well as sylvan fountains and rivulets (I shall enjoy myself with this lady).

12. This lady is dearer to me than my life. She is the sole lady of heaven who can easily be held by me. For her sake even the Devas lost their sense like groups of kings over Ramā (goddess Lakṣmī).

13. On hearing these words of his father, the prince of fine intelligence devoutly bowed down to the excellent king who was in the company of his step-mother and gave him much wealth for the sake of enjoying pleasures.

14. For the happiness of his father who was distressed, thanks to the activities of the fish-bannered deity (i.e. Cupid), he engaged men-servants who would comply with the commands and women-servants who had gold necklaces.

Thereafter, the son protected the Earth.

15. Dharmavibhūṣaṇa (i.e. Dharmāṅgada) was eulogised by the kings who surrounded him. He moved about in the whole of the Earth consisting of many continents. At that time, O king, (?) the people had no inclination towards sins.

47. If in this month one takes only one meal per day or takes food at night only, or takes only what is received unsolicited, the whole Earth consisting of a series of continents is obtained by the vow-observing men.

48. This month is said to be the bestower of devotion through Vratas, charitable gifts, worship etc. especially in the holy centre of Puṣkara, the city of Dvārāvatī and in Śaukara (Soron on the Gaṅgā near Itah).

49-50a. In this month the day of Hari is sacred; so also the five days called Bhīṣmapañcaka[1] (i.e. from the eleventh day to the full moon day of the Kārttika). If the Prabodhinī (wakening, the eleventh day or Ekādaśī called the "wakening of the Lord") day is spent by observing fast alongwith keeping awake at night, even a sinful man will never stay in the womb of a mother.

50b-51a. O fair lady, a person who sees a Maṇḍala (halo, disc of the sun) on that day attains the greatest region without having recourse to the systems of Sāṁkhya and Yoga.

51b-52a. O auspicious lady, by seeing Maṇḍala in the month of Kārttika, or Śūkara in the holy centre of Śaukara or by seeing Kokavarāha (the Boar incarnation of Viṣṇu) one does not become a son once again (i.e. one attains Mokṣa).

52b-53. O lady of unsteady side glances by seeing Maṇḍala or Śrīdhara in Kubjaka, men are liberated from the three types of sins. One shall avoid oil and honey in the month of Kārttika.

54-55. One should avoid meat in the month of Kārttika,[2] one shall also abstain from women in the month of

---

1. *Bhīṣma-pañcaka* is a special Vrata to be performed for five days from the Kārttika Śu. 11 to the Full moon day. The performer has to take three baths per day, perform *Tarpaṇa*, *Japas* or 108 times repetition of the *mantra*, *Oṁ namo bhagavate Vāsudevāya*, worship of Viṣṇu and *Homa* with the mantra *Oṁ namo Viṣṇave* and partake of the five components of *Pañcagavya* respectively on each day of the Vrata: feeding of Brāhmaṇas and giving of religious fees.

2. Abstinence from flesh-eating in Kārttika is regarded as equivalent to performance of severe penance for one hundred years (*Kṛtya Ratnākara* 397-99). Abstinence of meat-eating during the Bhīṣma pañcaka period is called *Baka-Pañcaka* (*Kṛtya-ratnākara* 425).

Kārttika. O gentle lady, in the month of Kārttika a person devoted to Viṣṇu shall avoid Niṣpāva (? the bran blown away by the winnowing siev). He shall instantaneously be liberated from the sins committed in the course of the year. By taking a meal once a day the devotee attains royal womb (i.e. is born in a royal family).

56. The foolish person who partakes a bacon in the month of Kārttika is cooked (or roasted) in the Raurava hell for sixty thousand years.

57-58. Having been liberated from it, the sinner is born as a rural pig that eats faeces. No man shall eat fish or the flesh of a tortoise or a dear in the month of Kārttika. O gentle lady, by eating flesh in the month of Kārttika one is born as a Cāṇḍāla. Even if one observes a minor Vrata, Kārttika destroys all sins.

59. The initiation undertaken in the month of Kārttika is destructive of births of men. Hence, one shall assiduously undertake initiation in the month of Kārttika.

60. O lady of beautiful thighs, every thing performed by one who has not undergone initiation is futile. A man devoid of initiation attains the womb of an animal.

61. The Kārttika Vrata shall not be performed at home especially on the eleventh day of the Kārttika month. A man who performs the Kārttika Vrata in a holy centre attains the region of Hari.

62. A man shall observe fast on the eleventh day in the bright half of the month of Kārttika and on the next day, in the morning, he should give auspicious pots whereby he attains the abode of Hari.

63-65. The conclusion of all the Vratas in the course of a year is laid down in smṛtis in the month of Kārttika. In the holy centre of Puṣkara marriages are seen performed even without insisting on Uttarāyaṇa (northern transit of the sun) and the auspiciousness of Lagna (astrological division of time) especially during these four days in this month, O lady of fair complexion. The connections entered into during that period cause the increase of sons and grandsons. Hence, O Mohinī, I shall perform the holy rite in the month of Kārttika

19. There is no mention about the movements of the planets in the Vedas:[1] there is no indication of the time that is endowed with purity; nor (can we find these things therein) viz. the increase and the decrease of the Tithis nor the decision about the Parvans (New Moon and full moon) or the position of the planets.

20. Formerly, these had been decided by means of the Itihāsas and the Purāṇas; what is not seen in the Vedas is observed fully in the Smṛti.

21. What is not seen in both of these is explained by the Purāṇas, as for example, the expiatory rites in the cases of killing. O beloved wife, it is like the medicine in the case of a seriously ill patient.

22-25a. (If the Purāṇas had not explained the expiatory rites) it would not have been possible to have purification from sins in one's own case or in the case of others. O lady of beautiful eyebrows, what is sung about by the Vedas, what is recounted by the Vādāṅgas (ancillaries) is explained in detail by the Purāṇas and Smṛtis. O fair-faced lady, the Purāṇas repeat often like this—"when the day of Hari has arrived, food should not be eaten, food should never be eaten." By disregarding the Purāṇas one will attain the womb of animal. Even if one has taken holy ablutions, even if he has perfect self-control he will not attain salvation if he disregards the Purāṇas.

25b-26. Who will not salute his father? Who will not worship his mother? Who will not go to Gaṅgā the holiest of all rivers. Who will eat food on the day of Hari? Who will slander the Vedas? Who will cause the downfall of a Brāhmaṇa.

27. Who will have sexual intercourse with another man's wife? Who will take food on the day of Hari?

28. O beloved one, there is no other sin for a creature of muddleheaded nature, than taking food on the day of Hari. O lady of bright eyes, it is the cause that makes one fall into the pit (hell) of Yama.

---

1. VV. 19-22 state what topics are not mentioned in the Vedas but are decided in Purāṇas. Hence their superiority in some respects.

Mohinī said :

29. "O Ghūrṇikā (the name of the female attendant) bring here immediately those Brāhmaṇas who are the masters of the Vedas. It is likely that on being convinced by means of their words, the king may take food."

30. On hearing her words she (i.e. Ghūrṇikā) brought Gautama and the other Brāhmaṇas who were masters of the Vedas, near Mohinī.

31. On seeing the Brāhmaṇas, the experts in the Vedas and the Vedāṅgas come, Mohinī who was interested in her own affairs saluted them in the company of the king.

32. O king, all of them had the refulgence of the blazing fires. They sat on seats made of gold.

33-34a. Gautama who was the oldest among them spoke these words :"O queen, we experts in the different branches of sacred literature who dispel all doubts, have come here, for the purpose we have been called by you."

34b-35a. On hearing the words of those (Brāhmaṇas), Mohinī the daughter of Brahmā, spoke to them who were engaged in doing what was impossible for others.

Mohinī said :

35b-36. The doubt here is whether this man is stupid or deficient in intellect (?) The king says—"I will not take food on the day of Hari." (But) this entire universe consisting of the mobile and immobile beings has food as its support.

37-38a. Even the dead persons, the Pitṛs (manes) in the heaven are delighted with cooked food. O excellent Brāhmaṇas, the Devas desire for cooked rice, the Puroḍāśa [sacrificial oblations with ground rice) of the size of Jujube fruit. Hence cooked rice is the greatest nectar.

38b-39. Even the hungry man takes a bit of rice in its mouth and enters its crevice with great strain. To whom does not the food appeal ? But this king does not eat cooked rice and other edibles, when the day of Hari has arrived.

40. He has forsaken his own holy duties and abides by other peoples' Dharma. It is but proper on the part of widows and ascetics to observe Vratas.

38. "Of what nature are the words you are going to speak which will cause sorrow to me ? In making my husband truthful, misery cannot be caused to me by any means. If it is done for the name of my husband, I am not distressed at my death, or at the death of my son or at the destruction of my kingdom.

39. If the wife is affluent but sinful, and hence, O fair-complexioned lady, the husband is miserable (it is proclaimed that) she will have a downfall (in hell).

40. That sinful lady falls into hell called Pūya (of foetid things) and remains there for seventy Yugas. Thereafter, she is born as female musk-rat in the Bhārata land for seven births.

41-42. Then she is born as a female crow and then a female jackal* and mungoose. After taking the birth of a cow, she becomes purified. O beautiful lady, she who does not give wealth she possesses or her own life for the sake of her husband, is born as a worm in the faeces. O splendid lady, after being released from the womb of a worm, she is born as a Kāṣṭhīlā[1] (plantain tree ?)

43. This happened during my girlhood days. A splitter of wood at my father's place was chopping the wood for fuel for a long time.

44. Inclined to play alongwith my girl friends, I went near him as he was splitting the wood.

45-46. O lady of fair eyebrows, there a worm was seen by me coming from between the wood. Its body resembled butter and it had the lustre of collyrium. It had the length of the little finger and the thickness of a finger. On seeing it fallen on the ground, a crow came there to peck at it.

47. Even as the hungry crow was about to peck at it with its beak, it was prevented by me instantaneously with a lump of clay.

***Śyāli* is a hyper-Sanskritisation of Pkt. *Siyāli*. SK. Śṛgālī.

1. A Prakritic formation in Sk. meaning "one who lives in a log of wood (*kāṣṭha*)".

48. O fair lady, it was let off by the crow that was thus hit; but it had been pecked at by the beak and wounded. It was not able to run away.

49. It began to tremble. It was about to die. But sprinkled with water a little, it regained its normal health.

50. Then O fair-complexioned lady, the Kāṣṭhīlā spoke to me in human voice. She addressed me by my name Sandhyāvalī, while I was in the midst of my friends.

51. "O splendid-faced lady in my previous birth I was the daughter of the sage named Sumantu who was omniscient. I was the wife of Kauṇḍinya.

52. I lived in Kānyakubja (Kanauj in U.P.). I was affluent, hence, very arrogant. I was the favourite darling of my mother, father and other kinsmen.

53. Then I was given in marriage to the noble-souled Kauṇḍinya who was born of a noble family, was celibate (lit. who had no physical contact with any other women) and befitting me in every respect.

54. Bed and other things were given to me by my father as dowry and present. Ten thousand gold pieces too were given to me at the outset by my father-in-law.

55. I was fully satisfied with the wealth obtained from my father as well as father-in-law. I had cows, buffaloes etc. I was endowed with affluence (wealth) and foodgrains.

56. I was liked by my parents-in-law and the common people, on account of my good conduct. In due course of time, my father-in-law, the knower of the real meaning of the Vedic texts, passed away.

57. Taking the dead body of her husband my mother-in-law entered the funeral pyre. Thereafter, my husband offered water libations to his parents and performed their Śrāddha.

58. Within two months of that, O gentle lady, my husband went to the Royal palace out of curiosity but was afterwards overwhelmed by love passions of the heart.

59. Beautiful courtesans in the prime of their youth were seen entering the royal palace by that Brāhmaṇa.

60. With gifts of profuse wealth two of them were taken from there and brought to his house. My evil-minded husband retained them in his house for dalliance.

Truth should not be spoken to women. Listen to the reason thereof.

60. In such directives as "Do not reveal to the woman (the extent of) the treasury", it prevents future faults. That is said to be the cause of Dharma which reveals the subtlety of Dharma.

61. That is called wedded life where the witnesses of marriage had been Kuśa grass, Brāhmaṇas, water, fire, Vedas, Earth, time, space and Devas.

62. The rite of acceptance is laid down in the celebration of marriage. If the woman and the man are consecrated by Brāhmaṇas, they are regarded as the teacher and the disciple.

63. Hence, the bride and the bridegroom are mutually related as teachers and disciples. No difference at all, even to the minutest extent, should be understood by a discriminating man as existing between these two.

64. The importance of women and employees is in accordance with the difference in rites. If there is the defect of contrariety (in relations etc.) anywhere, the cause of it is fate alone.

65-66. The entire universe consisting of gods, Asuras, and human beings is subservient to Fate. Fate is the accumulation of impressions of Karmas in the previous births. He who enjoys and experiences whatever comes to his lot, whether auspicious or inauspicious and behaves spontaneously with both, is called a quiescent person by the learned knowledgeable men.

67. A quiet person whose activity is based on the Truth enables the world to cross mundane existence. It is by knowing such and other details that my husband was prevented from falling into hell.

68. He was sanctified by me by preventing him from committing the sin of violating virginity. That is the help rendered by me. He has now attained the goal of the virtuous and lucky men after having been struck down by you.

69. My husband was helped by me who know the subtlety of Dharma. O excellent Brāhmaṇa, I have acquired merit (Dharma) in saving your life.

70-71a. What has been achieved by that Dharma? Know it properly from me. I who am born in the species of an ogress, I who have been the wife of a Rākṣasa, have now become a Brāhmaṇa woman who can assume any form, the reason being Dharma.

71b-72. Dharma is the wish-yielding cow (Kāmadhenu). Satisfaction is the heavenly Nandana park. Vidyā is the cause of salvation and Tṛṣṇā (insatiable thirst) is the river Vaitaraṇī. My husband who was about to fall into Vaitaraṇī has been redeemed by me.

73. O Brāhmaṇa, I have helped this fair-faced girl also because she has been placed near a person who is the highest of all castes. She will be your wife in her father's house.

74-75. I will be guarding her and you for ever enlightening you with Dharma. Before my contact you had a wife, O Brāhmaṇa, who will be born as a being in lower animal species. Later on, as a result of my blessings, she will be released.

76. O Brāhmaṇa, in my previous birth I was the most beautiful woman in the world well-known as Kandalī. I was the daughter of the sage Aurva.

77. By the power of penance I was born as one of a twin. My brother born along with me, was suppressed by Aurva himself for the cause of Dharma.

78-79. I was educated and given in marriage to Durvāsas. O leading Brāhmaṇa, it was a result of my previous Karman that I attained him as my husband. I quarrelled with my husband. Hence, I was cursed by him and reduced to ashes. As a little of my sins remained, I was born as ogress.

80. In that birth this brilliant leader of demons Gobhila was attained by me as my husband but he has been struck down by you.

81. O excellent Brāhmaṇa, in his youth he had incurred a curse "Your death will be initiated by your wife on account of a certain princess."

82. As a result of my previous Karman, I have been bereft of the nature of an ogress. Being powerful on account of the auspicious actions, I become your helpmate.

83. At the outset my husband abducted a virgin and I

73. Thereafter, soon after sunset my husband called me and immediately clasped me within his arms. He made me sit on the couch and kept me within his embrace for a long time.

74. Then he called the ogress and the princess and said : "Service to this lady's feet should be rendered by both of you with due devotion.

75. She had been my wife previously. Hence she is certainly the eldest and senior-most to both of you." Then at the instance of our husband, my feet were touched by those two ladies.

76. O lady of beautiful eyes, they eschewed (completely) the jealousy and malice originating from the feeling that I am a cowife. Then, my husband called the servants and spoke those words.

77-78. "O servants, whatever wealth had been acquired by me at the outset from the possessions of the Rākṣasa, whatever had been received by me when I wedded the daughter of the king, bring these things respectfully. Do not delay. This lady is the mistress of everything of those riches."

79-81. O splendid lady, at his words the wealth was immediately brought by the servants. My husband offered the entire wealth to me with love and mind untarnished by deception. He honoured me with ornaments and garments, even as the two ladies, the ogress and the princess were looking on.

82. O splendid lady, he kissed my lips and embraced me as I was seated on the couch. On seeing this wonderful dedication of his self and wealth unto me by my husband, (and on hearing) his words that thrilled me and (feeling excited) because his hands pressed my breasts, I fell down dead like a cow struck down by a sword. My vital breaths left me.

83. Then I attained the torture in the hell assigned to me by Yama. O splendid lady, after covering that period I experienced anguish and misery and was born as a Kāṣṭhīlā.

84-85. I shall have to be born in the animal kingdom thousands of times. O splendid-faced lady, the woman who does not dedicate her wealth and life to her husband will undoubtedly attain this state. By understanding this, one should save the wealth and life of one's husband.

86. Husband is both father and mother, wealth and life, preceptor and salvation.

87. With a great deal of merits the woman goes to the region of Viṣṇu alongwith her husband if her body is cremated alongwith him. But a woman greedy of wealth and of her body (?) attains Yama's torture and the affliction of being born in base wombs in lower species.

CHAPTER THIRTYONE

The Glory of the month of Māgha

Vasiṣṭha said :

1-4. On hearing the words of that Kāṣṭhīlā, the lady of pure smiles named Sandhyâvalī became extremely surprised and addressed her with respect. "O Kāṣṭhīlā, by your words I am much surprised now. Why at all did I happen to see you attaining the base mode of existence ? By what Karman can your liberation be effected from this base birth ? O, one of large limbs, please tell this to me. On seeing you I have become miserable. O excellent one, pity is roused in my heart, on seeing your body resembling a lump of meat that is smooth and comparable to a lump of butter.

Kāṣṭhilā said :

5. O lady of charming eyebrows, even if you are going to give the entire earth for my sake, I cannot all of a sudden extricate myself from this base birth.

6. O blessed lady, listen, I shall point out that holy rite (from which accrues merit) that bestows the great goal, whereby I can liberate myself from the bondage of Karmas.

7. What is called the month of Māgha is remembered as the most excellent of all months. In it, Brāhmaṇa-slaughter

to the red Aśoka flowers. I am absolutely obedient to you. I shall carry out some other purpose of yours.
I am subservient to you. O gentle lady, be pleased with me. Give me the alms in the form of my own son's life. A virtuous son is very rare to be obtained. The day of Hari (Ekādaśī) is a rare day of holy rites. Rare indeed is the water of Gaṅgā. Rare is a beloved mother on the Earth. Rare is the birth in a noble family. Rare is the beloved wife born of a good family. Rare is the charitable gift of gold. Rare is the facility to worship Hari. Rare is the initiation pertaining to Viṣṇu. Rare is the collection of Smṛti texts?

41-45A. Rare is the residence in the holy centre of Śaukara.* Rare is the opportunity to meditate on Hari; rare is the holy rite of keeping awake on the day of Viṣṇu; rare is the purification of the self (or getting honour to oneself); rare is the attainment of the birth of a son; rare is the holy water of Puṣkara; rare is the contact with virtuous eminent people; devotion is said to be rare; rare is the charitable gift of a Kapilā (tawny) cow; rare is the (facility to) set a blue (calf) free. O fair-faced lady, rare is the Śrāddha performed on Trayodaśī (Thirteenth day). Rare is the Earth (as an object of charitable gift). Rare is the observance of holy rite that destroys sins. O woman of sweet eyebrows, rare is the replica of cow made of gingelly seeds and given over to a Brāhmaṇa. O fair lady, rare is the bath with the embylic myrobalan. Rare is the day of Hari.

45B.-46. Rare indeed is bath in cold water at the auspicious time of the passage (Parva-kāla) of the moon, especially at the auspicious time of dawn in the month of Māgha. O queen, rare is the performance of a religious rite punctiliously in conformity to Śāstric injunctions.

47. Rare indeed is the wholesome diet and efficacious medicine that dispels sickness. Rare is the procedure along the path of scriptures.

48. Rare is the remembrance of Viṣṇu at the time of death, O fair-complexioned lady. Thus, O fair lady, carry out my words that protect Dharma.

---

*Mod. Soron on the Gaṅgā, 27 miles NE of Itah (U.P.). Viṣṇu in the Sūkara (Boar) form killed Hiraṇyākṣa here—DE 195.

49. O lady of beautiful limbs, of what advantage is the killing of my son to you? It behoves you to be pleased. The worldly pleasures have been duly enjoyed. The kingdom has been made free of thorns.

50A. I have placed my foot on the heads of those (i.e. surpassed those) who protect Devas, cows and Brāhmaṇas.

50B-51. A. I will never injure with my hands my son who is the object of my destiny."

Mohinī said :

52-53. Dharmāṅgada is not my enemy, nor do I kill your son. I have told you at the outset, "Eat on the day of Hari". O king, rule over the earth as you please, for many years. I do not kill your son. My object of accomplishment lies in your taking food. O king, I have no interest in the death of your son.

54. O king, if the son is dear to you, may the food be taken on the day of Hari. O king, of what avail are these laments which are beyond the pale of Dharma.

55-56. Keep the truth assiduously. Carry out my word. "Dharmāṅgada who was standing in front, observed Mohinī, the lady with slender waist, speaking thus. After bowing to her he said. It is this (here). Take it. Do not entertain any fear or suspicion, O beautiful lady.

57-60. He drew out his stainless glistenting sword and placed it in front of the king. He placed himself too in front of the king and said with a steady resolve in truth and virtue.

Dharmāṅgada requested :

"O my father, delay should not be made by you in striking me down. O king, make my mother's words true. Keep up your promise. The Ātman should be protected even at the sacrifice of wealth, wives or sons.

To a king who is desirous of welfare, the progeny is for the purpose of preservation of Dharma. Death for your sake is the bestower of ever-lasting salvation on me. You too will attain the pure worlds in virtue of your keeping of your own promise.

even though it is true that god Brahmā, the creator (of the universe), is the grandsire of the world and is worthy of respect and worship by all gods of whom Rudra was prominent.

31A-32A It was out of his affection for Mohinī (and for her consolation and pleasure) that god Brahmā got perplexed and presented his solution. O king, when a great work is at hand and if it is impossible to get it accomplished in the three worlds, the obeisance offered to a younger person is not censured.

32B-33. On seeing the creator of all the worlds arrived there alongwith the Devas, that Brāhmaṇa who was a master of the Vedas and the Vedāṅgas and who was absorbed in performing austerities, got up and bowed down to god Brahmā, those sages and the Devas.

34. With great devotion, he made all of them sit and eulogised the lotus-born deity. Then the lord and creator of the worlds, the preceptor of the universe became delighted.

35. 36A On behalf of Mohinī, they requested the Brāhmaṇa who had been honoured by the king before. "O dear one, O Brāhmaṇa of good conduct, O helper of the other world, O Ocean of mercy, please show some compassion. Be the bestower of salvation on Mohinī.

36B-38. O Brāhmaṇa, it was for deluding Rukmāṅgada that she had been deputed by me. She is my daughter. O bestower of honour, on seeing the world of Yama empty and Vaikuṇṭha full of unperturbed people this gentle lady, the benefactress of the Devas, was mentally created by me. O Brāhmaṇa, listen to what I am explaining to you.

39-40. The way of Dharma is very subtle. It brings about the welfare of the entire world. I had tested Rukmāṅgada through this lady who acted as the touch-stone. Thus along with his wife and the son, O Brāhmaṇa, he was enabled to attain Hari's abode through the unflinching and unobstructable devotion and the observance of fast on the day of Hari.

41-42. Yama's abode was made empty by the activity of wiping off the lines in the record of Citragupta—Yama's accountant of human deeds. O Brāhmaṇa sage, it is not proper on the part of a Kṣatriya to be critical and antagonistic to the

Devas. Particularly to the Brāhmaṇa they render great assistance.

43. It (the place in Vaikuṇṭha) is attained neither by the knower of Sāṁkhya, nor through the Yoga system consisting of eightfold paths. It is to be attained only through devotion. O Brāhmaṇa, the husband who was the king (Rukmāṅgada), the son (Dharmāṅgada) and the cowife (Sandhyāvatī) were enabled to reach it.

44. What she had done against the crestjewel of a king who was extremely meritorious was a sin by which she was cursed and reduced to ashes by your imprecations.

45. This woman strove for the Devas, for the increase of worldly existence and for rendering help to the king. She is not selfish. O Brāhmaṇa, how can she incur disrespect ? If at all there is any disservice on her part, kindly forgive it.

46. Be merciful, resort to tranquillity and quiescence, the grinding of the pounded flour (i.e. superflous exertion) is not justifiable. This woman was struck down by your cursing her. Be pleased. Be the bestower of salvation. O Brāhmaṇa, if this is performed, this Mohinī will eschew her cruel grudge against you, who are worthy of being worshipped."

47. On being urged thus by the lotus-seated deity, he (the Brāhmaṇa) thought intelligently and abandoned his anger. Then the leading Brāhmaṇa said to the lord of the Devas (Brahmā) who created the body of Mohinī.

48. "O lord, inasmuch as your daughter Mohinī is burdened with so many sins, she has no place in this world teeming with living beings.

49. "It is out cf my affection for you that I shall state before you what has been thought of by me after much critical deliberation in the case of Mohinī, and you are certainly worthy of respectful worship by me all the more.

50-53A O lord of Devas, I shall see that your words turn out to be true as well as those of mine. The affairs of the Devas and duties of Mohinī must go on. Hence let Mohinī stay in such a spot as has not been occupied by any

DPH Education Series

DISTANCE EDUCATION

U K SINGH • K N SUDARSHAN

DISCOVERY PUBLISHING HOUSE
NEW DELHI-110002

First Published - 1996

Reprinted - 2018

ISBN: 978-81-7141-337-9

Distance Education

Published by:

DISCOVERY PUBLISHING HOUSE PVT. LTD.

4383/4B, Ansari Road, Darya Ganj
New Delhi-110 002 (India)
Phone: +91-11-23279245, 43596064-65
Fax: +91-11-23253475
E-mail: discoverypublishinghouse@gmail.com
sales@discoverypublishinggroup.com
web: www.discoverypublishinggroup.com

Printed at:
Infinity Imaging Systems
Delhi

differentiated from the knowledge of the priests. In ancient Babylon the priests were physicians and teachers in one person. The Indian Veda consisted at first of hymns, teachers in one person. The Indian Veda consisted at first of hymns, prayers, wordings and proverbs which were important in sacrificial ceremonies. Only later varying systems of interpretation and research approaches developed out of them and disciplines like law, logic and dogmatics branched off. The Egyptian priest caste also imparted collections of hymns as part of the holy literature. There again,. the scientific disciplines could emancipate themselves from mythical ideas and ritual reinforcements only later. This applied of course, to the respective instruction as well.

In the beginning, however, the forms of instruction corresponded to sacral contents. Everything we still can learn shows us that the priest-teacher was venerated by the students and that the instruction and examinations were permeated by a ceremonial solemnity. Keay reports, for instance, how the opening ceremony of the instruction of Brahmins proceeded:

The student had to grasp with his right hand the left hand of the teacher-leaving, however, his thumb free - and to speak the words : 'Venerable Sir, recite!' In doing this he had to direct his eyes and his to the teacher. He must touch his head three time with kusa-grass and hold his breath for the space of fifteen moments. Then he had to sit down on the kusa-grass, the tips of which had to be bent in such a way that they point to the east. Then, five mystical words must be spoken. Another part of the daily ceremony was that the student embraced the feet of the teacher before and after the beginning of the instruction.

These activities were, as Keay explained, considered to be of great importance as they were to impress the students by 'their mysterious holiness'.

It is obvious that most forms of our present instruction have left those sacral origins far behind them, of course. However, on looking more carefully one can see that the process of secularization has not yet ceased everywhere. As distance education is mainly dependent on indirect interaction and communication it has, so to speak, completed its seculization. The interaction between teacher and student is objectified by rational teaching techniques and the use of technical media to such a degree that even relicts of archaic attitudes are no longer possible. In instructional face-to-face situations, however, one can still find them. In fact, rudiments of an originally sacred teaching-learning behaviour can be identified in the following circumstances:

- teachers - be they in the classroom or lecture hall - see themselves as the source of knowledge;
- the teacher dominates the students verbally in such a way that the intended dialogue between the student which is structurally similar to that of a priest in the pulpit preaching to the faithful;
- the students rise from their seats when the teacher enters or leaves the classroom;
- there are ceremonial greetings and forms of dismissal;
- the teacher - for example, in English public

education can be also used for secular purposes. There was a growing need for the establishment of town schools and of an urban education. In the era of the Enlightenment, teaching and learning were secularized even further. People were inspired by the image of the individual who is able to change unsatisfactory conditions of society by means of reason. For the first time reason was attributed to everyone. And there was an eagerness to educate people in such a way that they learned how to use reason in an efficient way. There was a widely published popular literature in the form of moralizing periodicals and scientific treatises at that time. The enlightened individual was to become emancipated. He was to learn 'to use his reason without the guidance of anybody else'. It is evident that teaching and learning received new directions in this era. For the hypothesis mentioned it is important to note that the inner relationship between instruction and practical and useful activities was seen. Instruction assumed a rational-utilitaristic meaning. Furthermore, it is remarkable that in people's conceptions of life, vocational efficiency and success in practical life became significant - an idea which was propagated in Germany above all by the philanthropic movement. Only then did it become possible for long-term systematical work in an occupation to be valued and considered to be a 'sense of life' and 'a standard for success in one's life'. Seemingly, this is one root of the motivation for vocational qualification which was to become so important for distant students in our time.

Further preconditions have been described by David Riesman in his theory of various constants of social behaviour which can be identified in European and American societal development. According to this theory, people in pre-industrial society were tradition-directed; that is, that their observation of the external rules of behaviour was regulated and forced upon them down to the last details by customs, habits, ceremonies, rites and etiquette. When society became industrialized, however, it developed entirely new mechanisms of maintaining conformity. In childhood or adolescence, people now internalized specific principles of the desired behaviour which took effect on the whole of their lives like a steering gear. In this way, types of persons emerged who succeeded in determining their lives without a strict and obvious direction by tradition. They became inner-directed. Only now did they become able to act on their own discretion. And only in the industrialized society did they have options of doing so, as traditions fragmented, many new goals of life emerged, and conditions of life changed increasingly. Those who intended to realize the career prospects provided by the new society had to learn to take the initiative and to disentangle themselves from tradition-directedness.

Whereas the tradition directed individual could not choose between work and spare time, as their lives were regulated by tradition with regard to this as well, the inner-directed persons had the possibility of separating leisure time from working time and being able to have it at their disposal. Under the influence of the Protestant success ethic this happened increasingly in favour of useful activities, for the endeavour to be efficient, to control oneself permanently and to fight the 'demon of indolence' was religiously motivated. The then change of dominant attitudes as a consequence of the transition from traditional to modern society. Parsons presented the following four pairs of alternative value-orientations:

Traditional society	*Modern society*
affectivity	affective neutrality
particularism	universalism
ascription	achievement
diffuseness	specificity

With the help of this catalogue it is possible to describe more precisely the characteristic traits of industrialized education proposed so far.

The above mentioned familiarity between teacher and students in the traditional classroom indicates that affectivity plays and important role in face-to-face teaching. Indeed, there the range of emotional relationships is wide as has been shown by many empirical studies of social interaction in the class room. On the other hand, distance education is normally characterized by affective neutrality - as here the teaching and learning is not achieved by an interaction of persons, but, strictly speaking, of isolated functions. As Fairs also suggested, this does not necessarily mean that technically mediated instruction cannot be affective at all. Now and then one can find initial stages of it. Generally speaking, however, it remains safe to say that in distance education the social relations tend to be neutral.

Traditional instruction in the classroom is oriented to a particular frame of reference : a given teacher teaches a given learning group in a given temporal and locational situation. Industrialized instruction, on the other hand, disregards particular conditions of this kind, as it has a more general, if not principally universal frame of reference. Distance education tends, indeed, towards universal application.

With traditional instruction in the classroom teacher and students orientate themselves to certain ascribed qualities. Students, for instance, are 'diligent', 'good companions', 'well-behaved', 'cheeky', or 'exercise restraint'. Teachers are 'strict, but just' or 'soft'. The orientation in this dimension may become more important than the original objectives of instruction. A proof of this is the student who is the best one with regard to his school work, but plays openly a peripheral part in the dynamics of the learning group. With industrialized instruction, however, students and teachers orientate themselves exclusively towards the achievements which are assessed with the3 help of tests.

Traditional instruction can be characterized by diffuse value-orientations. The reason for this is that the norms of the learning group and the experience of 'group life' are usually not considered and, therefore, made conscious to a slight extent only. They become effective in direct social interaction in a global-holistic sense. Correspondingly, the teachers often think that precise objectives of instruction cannot be described, the methods to be chosen cannot be predicted and the sequencing of instruction cannot be fixed in advance. In contrast to this, in industrialized instruction the indirect interaction is orientated towards the specific qualities of teachers and students in the sense that

saying that man is 'world-open', in the sense that he is not tied to his environment, not adjusted to adaptation, but rather to change. This means that he actively organizes his environment. In fact, he is 'the only being who is able to react to change of his environment and who is best in experimenting with it'.

Industrialized education must be seen as the result of such a basic disposition as well as of an epoch-making thrust in the development of mankind. Now, people face the necessity of coping with 'a new and greatly advanced situation'. If they employ industrialized forms of education they will surely have to bear grievous losses of traditional forms of life. But this happened again and again in the history of mankind whenever new media were used. The design and the implementation of further forms of industrialized education will also be risky. However, the difficulties to be expected are part of those critical developments typical for our time of transition from the last phase of the last western visualization to the first phase of the emerging global industrial civilization. This development may raise mankind to a high general level of civilization never reached before.

Seen anthropologically, man is also 'a being open for the future'. As such he will be able to overcome the critical structural changes which result from such transformations of civilization and in education especially from the juxtaposition of traditional occidental forms of instruction and the industrialized forms of teaching and learning in the coming world civilization. History has shown that 'man has repeatedly been able to overcome extremely advanced alienations which were caused by transformations of humanity'

The arguments of the critics of culture that the humanity of education is threatened by the use of rational planning and organization, and of technical media, no longer hold true in the light of this anthropological discussion. Seen in a larger context the construction of complex technical systems of teaching and learning and their successful implementation must be interpreted as a real proof of man's capacity to react to fundamental changes of society. It is a building block for the 'secondary environment' which people must create in order to survive. In the same way in which technology was not anything strange or even hostile to the inner nature of man in the anthropogenesis, their efforts to industrialize instruction, their ability and skill to instruct extremely large groups of persons with the help of technology can be interpreted as a condition for the possibility of survival in the forthcoming industrial world civilization.

content is carried by audio-cassettes or transmitted over radio and to which printed materials are peripheral, if used at all, have been used by distance educators. They are frequently cost-effective, can be used by people with literacy problems and may be a successful method of teaching languages. The University of Waterloo in Ontario is an extensive user of this method.

Video-based. Distance education can be video-based when the basic educational content of the course is broadcast on television or contained on video-cassettes. Some printed materials containing background, further reading and assessment procedures often are supplementary, to the course. The development of cable television and the possibility of home ownership or rental of VCRs make this an area of interest in some cultures.

Series of programmes for television have already been developed by a number of groupings in America and elsewhere and a series of programmes based on video-cassettes is offered for credit by the independent study division of the University of Minnesota. Such programmes are to be regarded as distance education when they satisfy the characteristics outlined in the first section of this article.

A variant of both audio and video-based programmes is the educational use of satellites. Daniel presented an evaluation of the first attempts at satellite-based programmes to the 11th World Conference of the I.C.C.E. at new Delhi. Interest has also been aroused by the educational programmes of the Appalachian Area Satellite Project.

Computer-based. A computer can be the medium on which educational programmes that fall within the definition of distance education are based. A number of institutions have developed computer-based distance education programmes and the Fall Education Company lists over 300 computer-based courses already developed for the ATO system. They range from Accounting Fundamentals to Zeiss - a model Planetarium. It is known that in America negotiations are in progress for the accreditation of some of these computer-based programmes for college and university credit.

No evaluation of the relative merits of the media described nor of the possibility of developing a multi-media system by combinations of the various components is offered here. Nor can consideration be given to whether it is possible or desirable to combine distance education with on-campus education. That is the work of other studies.

Institutional type

When consideration is given to the

— influence of an educational organisation especially in the planning and preparation of learning materials

— two major groupings of institutions can be distinguished: those that are privately sponsored and those that are publicity supported.

Private, proprietary correspondence schools have made valuable contributions to this field of education since the last century. In recent years standards have been set by affiliation to national accrediting bodies: the National Home Study Council of the U.S.A., the Association of Accredited

3 A Theory for Distance Education

Distance education has managed very well without nay theory. It has been used to bring education, through print, radio or television, to thousands and thousands who would never get to school or college. And, as practitioners, at the British National Extension College and at the International Extension College, we have shunned theory, arguing that we were interested only in practice. Partly that is policy—though one man's policy is another's prejudice - and a desire to keep out in the wide open spaces of educational innovation rather than creep into the house of theory, seen as an annex to the ivory tower of academe. Partly it is a reflection of our intellectual tradition: The British were never ones for theory in any case. We have always been empiricist, anti-metaphysical in philosophy, mistrustful of theoretical systems. And partly it is a suspicion of two kinds of theory—of those which try to simplify education to a theory as grand as E = MC and those who try to restrict it to a theory which 'is neutral with regard to ends but exhaustive with regard to means'.

But questions about the theory of distance

teaching will not go away. If we define distance teaching as 'an educational process in which a significant proportion of the teaching is conducted b someone removed in space and/or time from the learner', legitimate, general and therefore in one sense theoretical questions arise about the circumstances in which it is relevant. These questions are important if distance teaching is to be taken seriously as a set of educational techniques. They can be answered by references to theories of education and of communication.

If follows, then, that if we are to build a house of theory for distance education, its architecture will depend on existing philosophies of education, and theories of communication or diffusion; it will not be constructed from brand-new components. Within such limits it is possible to state a theory. For the sake of formality and to stimulate disproof, it is stated in the form of fourteen statements or hypotheses.

The statements depend upon political as well as philosophical views about education. In Distance Teaching for the Third World" we quoted Nyerere:

Man can only liberate himself or develop himself. He cannot be liberated or developed by another. For man makes himself. It is his ability to act deliberately for a self-determined purpose which distinguishes him from the other animals. The expansion of his own consciousness, and therefore of his power over himself, his environment, and his society, must therefore ultimately be what we mean by development.

So development is for Man, by Man, and of

4 University-level Distance Education

Introductory remarks

'Distance education' is a form of education in which the students of universities and institutes of higher learning do not attend regular classes or lectures, but instead study teaching material especially prepared for this purpose by professors and their staffs together with experts in distance education - and interact indirectly with members of the teaching staff by means of technical media for the guidance and control of their learning.

This means that the distance between the living space of the student and their Alma Mater is not the decisive characteristic. It is true that this understanding of distance is applicable to most distant students - but not to the great number of regular students living on the campus who attend classes and study 'at a distance' as well, for instance, at many US-American universities. The term 'distance', therefore must be qualified in the sense that it means in the first place 'not face-to-face'. This means that the students are not pinned down to fixed times, places and persons, but are free to decide themselves when, where, what and how they wish to study.

- *Type 3*: Distance education types 1 and 2 are supplanted by lectures and demonstrations on radio and television. This multimedia approach has been tested in the United States and England.
- *Type 4*: Distance education is organized in such a way that a programmed computer performs important teaching functions. The type has been tested by the US Air Force.

There are two special developments of distance education: *Combined distance education*: Here two or three forms of study, each of which could lead separately to graduation, are incorporated in such a why that they form a new teaching-learning structure. In East Germany, for instance, it is possible to combine traditional tuition on the campus with evening study and distance education.

Group distance education: A number of students enrol in the same course of distance education and meet regularly in order to recapitulate, check and discuss what the have learnt by reading the teaching material. They are often called 'self-help groups'.

Distant students

No accurate information is available about the number of distant students. The statistical data which have been found are partially incomplete, and refer to different years and to courses of different lengths. They will be specified here only in order to give at least some indication as to how large the groups of persons are which will be dealt with.

As distance study differs from country to

being higher than that of traditional methodologies for face-to-face teaching based on common sense, pragmatic approaches and didactic recipes. Nevertheless, wherever western universities insist on a careful development of written special materials for distance study courses and on a regular correspondence between teacher and student, they profit by these early experiences.

Eastern European models of distance education, however, are not related to this tradition. Consequently, little or no attention is paid to the development of special teaching and learning material and to the regular, individual correction of test papers. Mostly, these elements are substituted by regular consultation periods at weekends, and b yearly seminars of several weeks' length. This may be considered as an adjustment of forms of traditional university study to the conditions of distant students. It was made under the unfortunate socio-economic conditions of the time after World War II. Hence, many measures were dictated by sheer need. The students were urged to work in full-time employment and to study at the university at the same time. The universities had to rely on the professors and the further teaching staff as well as on the infrastructure at hand. they used the same curricula and the same text-books which were provided for the say students. Hence, one could define the eastern model of distance education as a system of administrative measures which enable the universities to cater for considerable numbers of additional students who were expected to study mainly at home. This, of course, means that the eastern model is not derived from any elaborated concept in which the elements of self-study, regional consultation periods and yearly seminars at the university are carefully related to one another. Gerhard Dietze, a leading expert in distance education at the University of Dresden, deplores, for instance, the fact that 'the general scientific concept of distance education is inadequate and that, so far, its crucial components and their interactions in view of optimal learning conditions have not yet been analysed at all'. And Andrej Kamiac, a Czechioslovakian expert, explained that in his country distance education was introduced and developed by the administration of the universities and not by experts in teaching methodology.

Technological model of distance education

Reports from the United States, Sweden and Japan, and the planning papers of the Open University in Great Britain,show that at present a third model of distance education is becoming discernible. It is characterized by the calculated use of modern technical media—for instance, television, radio, computer and telephone, as well as audio and video tapes. This development changes the structure of the teaching and learning process to such a great extent that it seems to be justified to speak of new form of distance education, which I should like to call for the time being the 'technological model'.

The structural change can be seen immediately if one realizes that the use of these technical media confronts the teachers with new and difficult problems, as the contents of teaching and the teaching functions have to be redistributed if they change from the use of predominantly one

On the other hand, the phrase 'text and context in curriculum' captures the dynamic of processes of social formation, some of whose traces can be read in curriculum, both as an historical artefact and as an historical force-shaped by and shaping history.

Lundgren suggested that the problem of curriculum could be thought in terms of social necessity of sustaining a society's basis of production through reproducing—passing on to rising generations—the knowledge, skills, practices and social relationships needed for production. He argued that curricula are one of the ways in which the gap between production and reproduction is bridged. People wanting to ensure the future of existing means and modes of production must select and decontextualize the knowledges, skills, practices and social relationships required for production from the context of production, then recontextualize these knowledges, skills, practices and social relationships in forms suitable to the needs, traditions and patterns of work of the settings in which reproduction occurs. The result of this process of selection, decontextualization and recontextualization are curricula. Curricula thus embody ideas about how production can be related, and about how rising generations can be inducted to the forms of life generations that have gone before. As such, curricula are important historical documents, providing evidence about the ways in which societies understand themselves—evidence about what aspects of production a society regards as so important that reproducing them cannot be left to chance.

According to Lundgren, the development of

curricula is a continuing struggle to develop 'texts' which adequately represent the knowledge, skills, practices and social relationships needed for production in the context of reproduction, thus bridging the gap between material production and social reproduction. On this view, the central problem for *curriculum* is thus *'the representation problem'* — the problem of adequately representing the knowledge, skills, practices and social relationships needed for production in forms which can be taught and learned. When a group or a society resolves this problem for itself by developing a curriculum, it reveals something significant about itself—it reveals the way it understands the relationship between production and reproduction, and the relationship of rising generations to previous ones. When people studying curriculum reveal these understandings, they begin to unravel a society's underlying theories about itself, its economy and its culture, about the nature of education and schooling, and about the relationships between them.

From this analysis, Lundgren argues, it follows that the central problem for *curriculum theory* is the problem of finding the theoretical means to interpret different curricula in different cultures and societies in different epochs — by interpreting them as texts which, in their own ways, for their own times and settings, reveal specific ideas and theories about how the specific needs and contexts of production (for example, in the economy) are thought to be related to the specific needs and contexts of reproduction (for example, in schooling). If every curriculum reveals a specific theory of the relationship between production and reproduction,

organization among curriculum workers for these issues to be addressed. These social relations of curriculum theorizing recover theory as an equally central concern for curriculum practitioners in schools and classrooms as for curriculum policy-makers and designers outside classrooms. This focus on the social relations of curriculum production was, of course, simply another reflection of the trend which had set the scene for the emergence of the 'Curriculum Theory' course. At one and the same time the course acknowledged the contested nature of the curriculum and asserted the legitimacy of the teacher's role in these contests. The pedagogy of the course was one which set out to draw this conflict and debate into the open, making it public through the *Course Journal*. The course thus put itself at odds with the conservative view of curriculum which assumed or asserted that curricula could and should reflect a social equilibrium, and it did so by making debate a material feature of the life of the course.

While the course was constructing this form of life for itself, however, there were important shifts taking place in the culture more generally, and the course was far from immune to them. The course had arisen from a context in which there had been a long struggle among Victorian teachers for a greater say in curriculum matters, and it aimed to extend that struggle to the domain of curriculum theorizing. BY the late 1980s, however, the course found itself operating in a very different climate, in which the achievements of teachers in their struggle towards greater control over their own curriculum practice were being eroded. There were increasing signs that the state was once again exerting a more active control over the construction and legitimation of curricula — for example, in the reconstruction of curricula to meet the demands of a changing economy.

In the view of the course team, the 'Curriculum Theory' course could not be regarded as immune from these more general shifts; in higher education, as much as in schooling, the state and the economy were imposing new demands on the curriculum. The 'Curriculum Theory' course, with its particular theoretical bias and pedagogical emphasis, could be a forum in which this shift could be addressed and interpreted. The confusions over the theoretical perspective adopted in the course and its relationship to the course pedagogy noted in Terry Evans' course evaluation can be understood quite concretely in addressing this confusion. The course team was committed to modelling critical and self-critical curriculum debate through the practice of the course. Unlike other courses whose curriculum is more 'closed', the 'Curriculum Theory' course aimed to remain 'open', to allow students to debate an explore issues. Perhaps for this reason some students found the course confusing. In coming to grips with such issues in its own pedagogy and its own curriculum, members of the course, both staff and students, attempted to explore formative ideas and value positions in a rapidly changing social context. In the next section we will return to explore this issue in more depth.

To summarize: in the volumes of the *Course Journal* over the five years from 1983 to 1987 there are numerous examples of work where people have managed to analyse and interpret a wide range of curriculum issues relating to different educational

6 Distance Teaching: A Contradiction in Terms?

It is sometimes said that there is nothing new about the concept of distance education, since it is possible to point to examples of the use of written material for educational purposes almost back to the beginning of written records and a clearly didactic objective is inherent in, for example, the Epistles of St. Paul. However, it is only in the twentieth century, and perhaps particularly in the last decade, that teaching at a distance has achieved international recognition and even acclaim. Consequently some have seen teaching at a distance as an industrialized form of teaching arising out of the new techniques which have been perfected in the twentieth century; others, while not denying the importance of the new technologies, have seen in the recent rapid growth of this form of reaching a reflection of the increased and increasing costs of conventional teaching which is very labour intensive and to which distance teaching offers, therefore, a seductive alternative.

What makes distance teaching popular?

In both developing and developed countries the possibility of supplementing or even perhaps replacing conventional teaching methods by teaching at a distance has had wide appeal. For the developing countries, where the supply of trained and competent teachers is often severely restricted, teaching at a distance materials can be produced by a small skilled group of teacher which set a standard of excellence capable of wide dissemination, by passing the need for training, in the first instance, a generation of teachers and thus significantly reducing the time scale for mass education. An example of this can be seen in India where the central government, with technical assistance from UNESCO, has been involved in planning an open school project at the secondary level based on the Central Board of Secondary Education and following a similar syllabus to the Central Board's conventional secondary schools. Such a system would not only cater for 'drop-outs' from the conventional system—a large and increasing number forced for economic reasons to abandon full-time education and seek employment—but also 'left-outs', since the conventional secondary education system is not equipped to cater for the increasing size of the school population. In the developed countries the motives for experiments in teaching at a distance are more complex and here, perhaps, the cost of employing teachers is a more significant factor, but it is worth noting that one of the three primary objectives of the state government of Nordrhein-westfalen in setting up the Fernuniversitat in Hagen was to deal with the fact that the conventional universities could not cope with qualified potential students. However, even in developed countries the lateral expansion of knowledge—the arrival of new subjects and new

possible responses, the discussion cannot be all embracing, so that this development must always fall some way short of perfection. However, the creation of this internal dialogue for the student within the material has been a significant element in changing the student from a passive to an active learner.

The standard teaching package, however well structured, cannot provide an individualized learning system for students. It is only the introduction of a human element which can adapt to the almost infinite variety of student needs. Hence, in distance teaching, and in particular in the Open University, we have witnessed in recent years the refinement of teaching by correspondence alongside the development of the carefully designed teaching package. The technique and the approach of the correspondence tutor are not always immediately grasped by those who have been engaged in the traditional forms of teaching. The correspondence tutor is that of a facilitator. This requires two things: the ability on the part of the correspondence tutor to convey through his comments advice for further study and the ability to perceive his student's present state of knowledge and conceptual framework, so that the advice may be as relevant as possible to the individual student. The tutor must offer comments which are considered, human, constructive and supportive. The formal nature of written comment which is not susceptible of the inflection, tone and pause of speech, renders it liable to misinterpretation. Clarity is essential. While much has been done to refine the art of correspondence teaching, it is, as yet in its infancy. It is clearly not the case that the skills of the traditional teacher can be adapted for correspondence teaching; rather three is a need for the development of new skills.

The Open University has combined its teaching package with an individual support system offered through correspondence tuition and a general and continuous academic support provided by a a tutor-counsellor, who is responsible for the progress of the individual student from entry into the University until graduation. This general service is supplemented by specialist tuition beyond the foundation level. The interrelationship of the package of materials with the student has been achieved through the agency of tutor-counsellors and course tutors. Individual contact can be, and often is made by telephone and by post.

A rationale for study centres?

But we have till not supplied a rationale for the study centre, and indeed we seem increasingly to be isolating it as superfluous and as an anachronism in a system which, as we have seen, can probably comprehend the subject matter and advice/support. The study centre has been used for a number of functions in various distance teaching systems. In some it has been seen as a viewing centre where replay devices may be used. In others it has been seen as a library resource centre. In some it has been seen as a locus for student interaction and self-help groups, a substitute for the conventional campus. In yet others it has offered a site for practical experiments or the use of equipment, such as computing facilities, which are essential to study, but which cannot be offered to the student at home without great difficulty. Finally, there are cases

quality, to a theoretically unlimited number of students. The rationalization effect of mass production becomes apparent here.

3 The rigorous application of organizational principles and means saves teachers as well as students unnecessary effort.

4 At some of the newer distance teaching establishments, modern means of technical support, such as film, television and electronic data-processing installations, have replaced teaching staff in certain areas of their work, in particular, in the fields of giving information and assessing performance.

5 Student work through a course which has been tested prior to going to print. This prevents misunderstandings and stops students from going in the wrong direction.

6 The quality of a distance study course can be improved, because its effectiveness can be monitored at any time by scientific methods.

If the number of students required in a society outgrows the number of university teachers available, rational thinking should be able to find ways and means of changing teaching methods in such a way that the teaching resources of the university teachers available are used to the best effect, quantitatively as well as qualitatively. Distances study can be regarded as a result of such endeavours.

The division of labour

The division of labour has played an important role in the sociological theories of the last 100 years.

Applied to the production processes it means that the work is split in the sense of 'dividing one complete work process into a number of elementary procedures', as described by Adam Smith at an early stage. With an extensive division of labour 'training periods become shorter, more people are able to carry out the work and wages can be lowered.

A result of the advanced division of labour is increased specialization.

Men are much more likely to discover easier and readier methods of attaining any object, when the whole attention of their minds is directed towards that single object then when it is dissipated among a great variety of things. It is naturally to be expected therefore that some one or other of those who are employed in each particular branch of labour should soon find out easier and readier methods of performing their own particular work, whenever the nature of it admits of such improvement.

Just as the division of labour is a precondition for the mechanization of work processes and for industrialization as a whole, it has made university study at a distance possible. The division of labour is the main prerequisite for the advantages of this new form of teaching to become effective. The principle of the division of labour is thus a constituent element of distance teaching.

The 'complete work process', which is split in distance teaching, consists of the teaching activity of the university lecturer: namely, the entirety of the measures he takes in order to initiate and guide learning processes in students. Initially, the two

is able to change them spontaneously during a lecture, whereby not all the changes in his teaching method need to be reflected. In distance teaching, however, most teaching functions are objectified as they are determined by the distance study courses as well as technical means. Only in written communications with the distance learner or possibly in a consultation or the brief additional face-to-face events on campus has the teacher some individual scope left for subjectively determined variants in his teaching method. In cases where a computer is used in distance study, even this opportunity is limited further.

The advantages of objectifying the teaching process in the form of a distance study course lie in the fact that the teaching process can then be reproduced, thus making it available at any time and, above all, that it can be manipulated. Without objectification distance study courses could not take place anywhere and at any time and be continuously improved.

The objectification of teaching practice in distance study is of particular importance in societies where, on account of an hierarchic structure of universities and colleges, the function of the provider of knowledge is combined in many academic with that of a holder of very great authority. As a result of this the relationship between student and lecturer is similar to that of subordinate and superior. As distance study has largely been freed from subjectivity, the process of providing knowledge is hardly affected by situations of this kind. In this context, distance study is particularly suitable for the further education of adults.

Concentration and centralization

The investment required for mechanized mass production involving the division of labour has led to large industrial concerns with a concentration of capital, a frequently Centralized administration, and a market that is not seldom monopolized.

In this context it is significant that some distance teaching establishments cater for very large groups of students. The largest universities teaching at a distance in the USSR and in South Africa have over 40,000 students, and the Open University in England has more than 70,000. Each of these three establishments - as well as their Spanish equivalent - caters for the national demand. Obviously, a minimum number of students is necessary to make the technical installations and the establishment of an efficient organization feasible. Economically, it is therefore more worthwhile to create a large central distance study establishment rather than ten or twenty small regional institutions. Just as the industrial markets for certain products have long expended beyond narrow regional frontiers, such centralized distance teaching establishments must cross the traditional areas of the responsibility of universities and the educational administration.

If all the said principles of distance teaching are rigorously applied, monopoly-like prestige positions in teaching activity are created for leading experts in various disciplines. Just as no record producer would use a mediocre singer when he can engage a Fischer Dieskau, a distance teaching institution has to try and gain the best lecturers in their field for the development of its distance study courses. Just as in industry, however, one must ensure that such

groups to large groups must be seen as a perversion f an educational concept, one can, one can understand it if various governments see distance teaching, on account of its similarity with the mass-production process, as a means of providing very large groups of students more adequately with academic teaching than conventional methods would allow.

Indeed, the multiplication effect achieved by technology and the postal delivery system means that the university teacher and the distance learner —like producer and consumer -no longer need to live in the same geographical location.

From an economic point of view, the production of distance study courses represents mass production. Apart from reasons of profitability, the large number of courses produced forces distance teaching organizations to analyse the requirements of potential distance learners far more carefully than in conventional teaching and to improve the quality of the courses. Most American distance study courses are revised and re-issued at regular intervals. As American universities charge fees to cover the greatest part of the budget allocated to distance teaching departments, the quality of distance study courses must not be allowed to deteriorate. When, on account of mass production, the University of California has more distance study courses to offer than there is demand for them, it occasionally places advertisements for students in newspapers.

Statistics prove that the number of graduates in areas without a university is lower than in areas near universities. It is possible that, according to the principle of mass production, distance teaching will one day equalize the opportunities to study, just as industrial mass production has assimilated consumer patterns in town and country. Analogous to the increase in the standard of living, this would make a general increase in the level of education possible, which might not otherwise have been achieved.

Preparatory work

In a production situation where a division of labour prevails, economy, quality and speed of the work process depend on the right type of preparation. This is necessary in industries producing a type of preparation. This is necessary in industries producing a variety of articles and needs to be carried out by senior specialist staff in special departments, as workers, foremen and masters involved in the production process lack the necessary knowledge and experience. During the preparatory stages one determines how workers, machines and materials can usefully relate to one another during each phase of the production process. In addition, there are developmental and constructional tasks. The more thorough the preparation, the less is a successful production process dependent on the particular abilities of the workers involved. Consequently, workers can easily be exchanged. Normally, considerably larger sums of investment are required for preparatory work than was the case previously in the manufacture of goods.

As distance teaching institutions have to develop a great variety of distance teaching courses, the comparison with a firm producing a variety of goods comes to mind. In distance teaching too

live predominantly in rural areas - although this is widely assumed as there is usually a lack of specialized schools in country areas. On the contrary, they typically dwell in big cities and overcrowded industrial regions. It is only there that many differentiated possibilities for employment and promotion prospects inspire the students to learn, that the competitiveness of industrialized production urges them to take the initiative, and that the urban environment and atmosphere provides for additional incentives.

Most students are between twenty and thirty-five years old, which means that they are adults. Their educational standard is, as a rule, above the average of the respective age group - and not lower, as again is often assumed by those who consider instance students as disadvantaged persons.

What are the motivations of distant students? The strongest one is certainly the ambition to climb socially, to change from a blue-collar job to a white-collar job. They seek economic security. This motivation is activated when the students have clear ideas of the job they want to have and when the competence they have developed so far will help them to reach it. Furthermore, this motivation is supported by the fact that these students are adults who are able to judge their life chances more realistically than, say, students in secondary schools. They are conscious of the importance of their educational goals and of the consequences of reaching them.

There might be more hidden motivations. Some students decide to engage in distance education in order to protest against their parents who insisted on certain vocational training for their children. Through distance education they want to remedy early wrong decisions. The 'ambitious wife' can also be a powerful source of motivation. Sometimes, there is a revolt against discrimination in their daily work which distant students hope to escape by striving for better jobs. The great number of distant students in developing countries can perhaps be explained by similar motives.

The advertising departments of correspondence schools systematically exploit such motivations and reinforce them by creating an image of distant students which is certainly far beyond reality but nevertheless appeals to them. According to them, distant students belong to the 'intellectual elite' of the work force, have 'better chances' when applying for a new job, obtain a 'higher income', enjoy 'more prestige' and look forward to a 'happy future'. Sometimes the advertisements contain pictures under the headline: 'Formerly an employee with a low income - now a leading personality', showing all those present at a meeting of directors listening attentively to the former distant student. Another picture visualizes the success of the distant student who himself, travelling with an attractive young wife in a large sports car in a holiday paradise, is obviously able 'to afford anything'. The distant students will, of course, lower their sights depending on their maturity and life experience. But more or less subconsciously such advertisements may encourage them in their striving for success.

The motivations of distant students are also influenced by the way in which they are looked upon by society. This differs considerably from country to

Third, Willmott had a very firm view of the quality of course content he wished to achieve and was determined that the course materials should be both attractive and accessible to students. Those who became members of the core shared Willmott's perspective and were prepared to ensure that his view of the quality of the proposed course prevailed.

Fourth, dissatisfaction with the first contributions to the materials produced under contract reinforced the growing view of core members that quality would come from exercising much greater group control over the drafting of course materials than contracting allowed. Perhaps too much had been expected of contract authors working in isolation. This further constrained participation in the group working on the award.

Fifth, the actual drafting process adopted under the notion of group responsibility was intimidating, particularly as participants had little or no experience of the elements of peer appraisal it involved. This ma have simply been too threatening for some. While the core team came to value and even enjoy the group review process, it was stressful for those who made early contributions. Despite attempts to handle the review of materials in a sensitive manner, it was simply the case that the core were using a process they had adjusted to over time and which, for others, was more direct and critical than they may have expected. Further, through their shared experience core team members had reinforced personal friendships and the normative commitments they had to the programme. Critical exchanges were less likely to threaten them as individuals.

The stress for newcomers to the review process was exacerbated by the speed at which the core team worked. Consciousness of limited time was ever present, and with experience the group became skilled at collective editing under pressure, often working and making shared decisions at a rate which others, new to the group, could not match and found disconcerting. In part, of course, the core team had developed shared understandings and communication short-cuts which made their work both more efficient and less accessible to an outsider. In retrospect, this seems a critical component of the kind of creative process under study.

The notion of collective responsibility involved an understanding that decisions about the programme would be group-based. Further, the team would all be designers, authors, editors, transformers, teachers and administrators of the course. Two comments are necessary here. First, within this collective model some members had special responsibilities, for example, Luke acted as a team member and then subsequently undertook final editing responsibility. Similarly, the course coordinator was officially responsible within the College structure for administration of the course and often had to take decisions with minimal consultation, although these were rarely contested because of the shared perspective of the group. The Coordinator also chaired meetings and was expected to exercise some leadership within the team. Second, the roles fused over time. Members became adept at incorporating design and transformation considerations into their own writing and in the group review of draft material.

diagrammatic representation suggested a simplicity and linearity of approach which might better have been avoided, although the text stressed the complexity of issues, their diverse interrelationships, and the problematic nature of course development decisions.

Two comments should be made the application of this model to development of the Graduate Diploma. First, it was very much a reflection of the kind of deliberations involved in preparing the first development process. Secondly, the consideration of problems and generation strategies for dealing with them at no stage conformed to the sequential scenario offered in the model. Rather, decisions were taken in the light of a range of concerns which frequently cut across a number of the identified problem areas.

Instructional design in distance education

Because of the theoretical stance outlined above, the course team did not want unit on instructional design. It was included in the award at the insistence of the Accreditation Committee. Initially nobody wanted to draft the materials. In the attempt to find solutions to our own discomfort, some quite bold design decisions were taken. These also addressed other issues.

For the first time we were confronted with the certain knowledge that some part of our clientele would have considerable expertise in the substantiative area of the module and it would be necessary to accommodate hugely different levels of sophistication between students. Further, the team were strongly of the view that any approach to designing distance education which did not have a focus on the preparation of print materials ignored the realities of the field. This tool us well outside conventional instructional design approaches but was in strong accord with the transformational principles of MacDonald-Ross and Waller which had assumed considerable influence in our thinking about the course.

The design strategy adopted involved the preparation of three discrete sections. The first was intended for students who sought a good, standard introduction to instructional design or those with some experience of the field who wished to pursue an interest in the area. The section had two distinct strands to meet these different needs. The first strand was twenty-page guide to an introductory text. the second comprised a series of resource papers and readings designed to extend students' analyses of key debates and alternative view points about aspects of instructional design. The second section looked at the way instructional design was undertaken and considered by five distance education practitioners. It consisted of audio-taped interviews with the five, questions on each, tape transcriptions and a general commentary on the interviews. 'Practising Instructional Design in Print' was the third section and covered planning, writing, transformation, review and editing, binding, packaging and assembly of print materials. It was print-based, with a tape-slide presentation and a display of sample print-based materials prepared by individual practitioners which demonstrated a range of cheap, non-technical strategies requiring little professional expertise.

Thus far the decisions were legitimated not by recourse to rules of produce, as in the instructional design approach, but by a view of what constituted appropriate behaviour for tertiary teaching staff, which affords a more comprehensive, subtle and sophisticated basis for judgment. Nonetheless, whatever its refinement, the curriculum approach still establishes what will count as valuable knowledge and appropriate ways of acquiring it within the constraints of the expertise of the academic staff involved.

What Anne Forster was asking us to contemplate, and what the rest of us gradually came to understand and value, was that if you believe that the knowledge of the field rests with the experienced practitioners, then determining what is important to study cannot be dissociated from practitioners and the context in which practice is displayed. This becomes a real problem when designing a course for practitioners in diverse fields and with a range of professional interests. Practice is difficult to talk about without contextual knowledge and 'thick' description. Understanding comes from the meanings found in the practice of 0mature and experienced professionals when comprehensively described and subjected to informed reflection. It does not easily lend itself to the establishment of commonalities and prescriptions which are inter-contextual.

The test of a course like the Graduate Diploma must be the extend to which it endorses this approach to understanding through its own practice, while continuing to serve the other purposes for which it is also established, for example, certification of achievement. As such, decisions which address different ends must not become simple compromise. Our stance changed, the course team relinquished a considerable part of its control of what and how students should learn. The team determined to use its expertise to negotiate with and support students as they sought to find meaning in their own professional actions or in the institutional practice with which they were familiar. In the *Student Support* and *Distance Education Project* modules this new goal was achieved to a significant degree.

it can be quite hard to 'step back' and get a global view. One danger, therefore, is that as the experiments consist of very structured steps, they can be followed and yield the correct answer without a deep understanding of the process being developed. There was some evidence of this happening in the study. It seems that it is important therefore to consider not only how the material is presented but also the domain and the task involved.

The "Microcomputers in Schools' awareness pack was very successful. The same design was followed by the next level of pack—aimed at students with some experience of microcomputers.

Later course have evolved their own particular styles of teaching and methods of instructional design. There is no one design philosophy at the OU to which all course teams adhere, although the course-team model ensures that each course is exposed to considerable comment and feedback during its development. The approach to teaching practical work in courses within the Home Computing Policy varies considerably. However, if they are introducing students to new applications, most include step-by-step guidance plus commentary, although the level of detail and support will vary, as shown in the following examples. It takes students through from the very beginning and even includes a photograph of the keyboard. In this respect it is reminiscent of the detailed hand-holding guidance given to the students of the "Microcomputers in Schools' awareness pack.

In this section students are being introduced to Cosy MAIL—the MAIL facilities for the computer-conferencing system on this course. A Brief overview of the purpose of the exercise is given, followed by numbered instructions for the student to carry out. At the end of the third step there is a commentary. Note that the typography and layout carry quite a lot of information. The numbered steps help to reduce the cognitive overload by allowing the learners to see where they are quickly. Everything that appears on the computer screen is in bold type, and the commentary section is prefaced by its own icon.

The next example is also taken from the same course, but is rather different. Here, the learner has just found out how to select a desktop function by single clicking the mouse, working with GEM desktop program. Next, double clicking is introduced, and here a screen image is given so that the learner can check whether the action has been carried out correctly.

Students with differing amounts of experience will also need a different approach. One approach used in the technology foundation course, where it is reasonable to assume that most students are novices with respect to computing, is to introduce the operating system and the applications through audio-cassettes. This reduces the number of physical items students have in front of them, which can be a real problem. It also means the learner does not have to keep alternating between referring to a book and looking at the screen. The instructions on the audio-tapes were recorded in 'real time', so the student can carry out the instructions whilst

he provided, albeit never overtly, that I could have explored this new and emerging field of International Relations and India within it.

To both these men in my life I owe a great debt.

Jyotsna R. Bapat

1
Introduction

A crisis challenges an existing paradigm. The lesson from a crisis is, it is completely unpredictable. Which new paradigm will emerge, is unknown. Especially after the global crisis of COVID-19 the resulting paradigm shift was equally unpredictable, but worked out well for India. Since 2014 India had been experimenting with its Foreign Policy. Various actions were taken by Government of India to create a new 'neighbourhood first' foreign policy that prioritized its immediate neighbours in Indian ocean and Pacific Ocean for trade and development partnerships, developing military partnerships with developed nations focusing on its strengthening its military and particularly its navy, and sending a firm message to its unfriendly neighbours and terrorist attackers. All these policies created the space, for India to emerge as a significant Global Political leader supported by its neighbouring partner countries and friends, post COVID-19* when the old paradigm shifted and new one started emerging.

Globally the Sustainable Development Paradigm was the only dominant paradigm that was seen as a path to economic development and growth for a nation state. The assumption, on which it was based, was free trade and goods movement across states. But when a crisis happened this dominant paradigm

---

*Corona Virus Disease–2019, acronym–COVID-19.

from the experiences of various other prominent models, such as those of USAID and DFID. Learning from prominent bilateral donors, an administrative set up: Development Partnership Administration (DPA), was created as an integral part of the MEA. Like other donar country models, DPA does not formulate any development assistance policies, but deals with their coordination and monitoring. India's development assistance takes one of three forms: grant assistance, lines of credit, and capacity building. These Development Partnership Funds are closely linked to India's foreign policy and strategic interests in commerce and economy, energy security, food security, and search for natural resources and defence interests[6]. Not being an independent agency, the DPA has no officially-established 'vision, mission or procedures' or annual budgets. What has evolved in development assistance given by India to other countries, is funding that is dependent on the geo-political and security interests of the time. Currently outputs and outcomes of development assistnce are not transparently published in the public domain.

Model for Development Assistance Partnership

The Indian model of development partnership is comprehensive and involves multiple instruments including grant-in-aid, line of credit, and capacity building through technical assistance. Depending on the priorities of partner countries, India's development cooperation ranges from commerce to culture, energy to engineering, health to housing, fintech to infrastructure, sports to science, disaster relief and humanitarian assistance to restoration and preservation of cultural and heritage assets[7].

India's approach to development partnership is evolving. A largely human-centric approach marked by respect, diversity, care for the future, and sustainable development, its fundamental principle is cooperation, respecting development partners, and being guided by their development priorities. India's development cooperation does not come with any conditions, as stated by the Hon'ble Prime Minister of India in his address at the Parliament of

Uganda in July 2018. "Our development partnership will be guided by your priorities. It will be on terms that will be comfortable for you, that will liberate your potential and not constrain your future.... We will build as much local capacity and create as many local opportunities as possible, " said the Prime Minister[8].

The DPA, it has laid down a process for handling multiple instruments for fund allocations, including grant-in-aid, line of credit and capacity building and technical assistance. Existing ranks within the MEA are assigned to carry out these processes to DPA.

G7 Strategies for Aid and Investment

The MEA had sought to learn from the experiences of various other prominent models for ODA[9] to create the DPA as an integral part of itself. In 2012, the DPA was formed. It was decided that the best way to learn how to proceed further was to look at the global experience of the G7 countries, who have similar initiatives, and study their present and ongoing strategies in developing countries, with an especial focus on India's experience with them.

G7 is an inter-governmental organization that was constituted in 1975 and it is made up of democracies that are the world's financially largest, developed economies. The G7 ODA strategies, especially as used with regards to funding projects in India in the past, are similar to each other and they themselves do not take any development aid from other countries. In 2011, China had stopped bilateral aid. In 2017, India declared that it would not accept bilateral foreign development aid from any country.

Until 2016, all the G7 countries except Italy had their ODA[10] funded bilateral projects in India. They provided bilateral grants termed as 'Soft-loans' and technical assistance to various infrastructure and social development projects in different regions of India, more recently routed therough state governments to cities in India. Bilateral loans, also called concessional loans, are loans given by sovereign states. They consist of 25 per cent of grant element to donor countries[11].

World Bank Environmental and Social Framework (ESF)

The ESF of World Bank comprises a vision, a policy, ESF standards, and a governance mechanism, for a project funded by the World Bank.

- A Vision for Sustainable Development which lays out the Bank's aspirations regarding environmental and social sustainability. The two vision goals of *environmental and social sustainability* emphasise the importance of economic growth, inclusion and sustainability, including strong concerns for equity. Environmentally sustainable growth ensures climate change mitigation and adaptation to ensure wise use of finite resources, without compromising the future of following generations. Social sustainability ensures social development and inclusion of all communities impacted by the development project.
- The World Bank Environmental and Social Policy for investment project financing sets out the mandatory requirements that apply to the Bank. At a project level, this translates into development opportunities for all, particularly project impacted communities and conservation or preservation of natural resources and ecosystem services.
- The Environmental and Social Standards set out the mandatory requirements that apply to the borrower and projects. There are ten Environmental and Social Standards that each borrowing country has to establish for themselves and the project, to be met throughout the project life cycle, as per the sustainable development goals.

Environmental and Social Governance

- Local governance mechanisms of the borrower set environmental standards and social standards that are mandatory requirements as conditionalities for receiving finance. This implies that borrowers may set any additional standards that are country specific, so long as they do not contradict these ten standards. Governance mechanisms of the borrower are to be used and enhanced to support collaboration and create a grievance redressal mechanism that includes the judiciary, if needed.[8]

Asian Development Bank

The Asian Development Bank, as part of the World Bank, follows the World Bank guidelines on the environment and social security framework.

Safeguard Policy Statements (SPS) of ADB

The Safeguard policy of ADB has the following structure:

(i) SPS describes common objectives of ADB's safeguards.

(ii) Lays out policy principles, and outlines the delivery process for ADB's safeguard policy. The SPS is designed for application to current and future lending modalities like private financial institutions and caters to the varying capacities and needs of developing member country clients in both the public and private sectors.

(iii) Through their due diligence, review and supervision, ADB staff will ensure that borrowers/clients comply with a set of specific safeguard requirements that they are expected to meet when addressing social and environmental impacts and risks during project preparation and implementation. Over time, ADB may adopt additional safeguard requirements or update existing requirements to enhance effectiveness, respond to changing needs, and reflect evolving best practices.

(iv) A consolidated *Operations Manual* section that specifies ADB's internal review procedures for due diligence and for supervision throughout the project cycle.

ADB has three safeguard statements that are consolidated into this policy. These safeguard statements are related to the—

convert a two lane into a four lane transport and transit corridor between them, that would facilitate movement of goods service and people.

The Trilateral Highway would run from Moreh in India to Mae Sot in Thailand through Bagan in Myanmar. The border posts for regulating and facilitating movement of cargo and passenger vehicular traffic would be at Moreh in India and Mae Sot in Thailand, protocol for which is in the making. The Trilateral Highway represents the most significant step in the establishment of connectivity between India and the South East Asian countries.

Ensuring project continuation: While this project was being implemented, Myanmar, in 2014, expressed its inability to continue participation in the project on financial grounds and backed out of its commitment. India then offered to expedite the project by taking over the commitment of complete project and offered to take on the construction of the road.

Since 2017, India has taken on its construction of two sections of the Trilateral Highway in Myanmar, namely:

(i) Construction of 120.74 km Kalewa-Yagyi road section.[18]
(ii) Construction of 69 bridges along with the approach road on the 149.70 km Tamu-Kyigone-Kalewa (TKK) road section.[19]
(iii) Both these tracks pass through the mountain ranges and hill slopes and through rain forest with indigenous settlements along the way.
(iv) Private enterprise partnership with the government for trans boundary projects is standard operating procedure (SOP) for such ventures, going by other development aid funding agencies.

The work on both these sections were awarded on Engineering, Procurement and Construction mode, in May 2018 for the Kalewa-Yagyi section and November 2017 for the TKK section. The scheduled time for completion of both the sections are three years from the date of commencement at the project site by the executing agency.[20]

The funds released by Ministry of External Affairs through its DAF is $24.47 mln. (Rs. 188.32 crore) out of the approved cost of $197.34 mln. (Rs. 1459.29 crore) for the Kalewa-Yagyi road section (to be completed by 2021) and $0.65 mln. (Rs. 4.84 crore) out of the approved cost of $50.25 mln. (Rs. 371.58 crore) for the 69 bridges along with approach road on the Tamu-Kyigone-Kalewa (TKK) road section to be completed by 2023. Both the projects are being funded by Government of India under grant assistance to the Government of Myanmar.

The contracts for the projects have been given to Indian companies. This will be followed by a tripartite agreement for motor vehicles, with protocols for regulating and facilitating movement of cargo and passenger vehicular traffic, subsequently.[21] India is sensitive to indigenous communities and their needs as well as the need to conserve local forests, fauna and flora. There was a delay in project in the construction phase of the project, as the local indigenous community in a settlement wanted a realignment of the road construction.

Environment and Social Security Impacts

The two road projects are mainly an expansion of existing roads and building of new bridges parallel to existing bridges. But both these roads pass through mountain ranges and tropical monsoon forests and affect indigenous communities occupying the buffer zones of these forests.

The SoP for the construction phase of projects that India is involved in requires environment and social sustainability, and impact assessment, monitoring and mitigation as these involve sensitive ecosystems and indigenous communities. India reviews the ESSIA status at the construction stage and prepares mitigation action plans which involve mid-project reviews, if demanded by indigenous communities, sometimes causing delays in project implementation.

Currently, what is missing at the DAF funding phase is this environmental sustainability dimension. This leaves India

6. (UN Conference on Sustainable Development: REGIONAL FORUM ON ENVIRONMENT AND HEALTH IN SOUTH-EAST AND EAST ASIAN COUNTRIES' https://www.unenvironment.org/explore-topics/environmental-rights-and-governance/what-we-do/supporting-2030-agenda/implementation)
The 'Agenda 2030- The future we want' (https://www.unenvironment.org/explore-topics/environmental-rights-and-governance/what-we-do/supporting-2030-agenda/implementation)
7. (https://www.undp.org/content/undp/en/home/sustainable-development-goals/goal-9-industry-innovation-and-infrastructure.html)
8. (2016. "World Bank Environmental and Social Framework." World Bank, Washington, DC.)
http://pubdocs.worldbank.org/en/837721522762050108/Environmental-and-Social-Framework.pdf)
9. (Safeguard policy statement 2009. ADB Policy document. Asian Development Bank. Manila.
https://www.adb.org/sites/default/files/institutional-document/32056/safeguard-policy-statement-june2009.pdf)
Operational Manual Bank Policies. OM Section F1/BP Issued on 1 October, 2013 Page 1 of 2.
https://www.adb.org/sites/default/files/institutional-document/31483/om-f1-20131001.pdf
10. AIIB: Environmental and social framework. Approved February 2016 (Amended February 2019) March 2019 Asian Infrastructure Investment Bank https://www.aiib.org/en/policies-strategies/_download/ Final-ESF-Mar-14-2019-Final-Penvironment-framework.pdf
11. Amb (Retd.) Achal Malhotra, India's Foreign Policy: 2014-19: Landmarks: Priorities and Challenges Ahead, Central University of Rajasthan, July 22, 2019.
(https://www.mea.gov.in/distinguished-lectures-detail.htm?833#:~:text=The%20main%20and%20first%20and, national%20interests%E2%80%9D%20is%20fairly%20wide.)
12. The life cycles of projects include the following stages: pre-planning, planning, construction, operation, and end of programmme monitoring.
13. The National Environment Policy, 2006
https://www.india.gov.in/national-environment-policy-2006
https://ibkp.dbtindia.gov.in/DBT_Content_Test/CMS/

Guidelines/20190411103521431_National%20Environment%20 Policy, %202006.pdf
MoEFCC as nodal agency: http://moef.gov.in/rules-and-regulations/environment-protection/
(Bikram Kumar Dutta, Sanhita Bandyopadhyay 2010 Environmental Impact Assessment and Social Impact Assessment—Decision Making Tools for Project Appraisal in India World Academy of Science, Engineering and Technology 39 2010 pp 1116- 1121 http://rlarrdc.org.in/images/Environmental%20Impact%20Assessment%20and%20SIA.pdf

14. Ali Paka, Manuchehr Farajzadehb, _ Iran's Integrated Coastal Management plan: Persian Gulf, Oman Sea, and southern Caspian Sea coastlines, https://www.sciencedirect.com/science/article/abs/pii/S0964569107000166
15. Chabahar Port: https://en.wikipedia.org/wiki/Chabahar_Port.
16. Environmental Impact Assessment Studies for Development of Sea Port at Tadadi, Karwar, Karnataka Sponsor Karnataka State Industrial and Infrastructural Development Corporation Ltd., Bangalore, CSIR-National Environmental Engineering Research Institute Nehru Marg, Nagpur- 440 020 August 2014
http://kspcb.gov.in/PH/KSIIDC_EIA%20Report_23032015.pdf
17. (Ministerial meeting 23 Dec 2003- media centre https://www.mea.gov.in/press-releases.htm?dtl/8948/ministerial+meeting+on+trilateral+highway+project+among+indiamyanmarthailand+on+december+232003
18. *Ibid.*
19. *Ibid.*
20. *Ibid.*
21. Shri Mansukh L Mandaviya, MoS, Road Transport & Highways gave this information in 'Reply to Lok Sabha question (Press Information Bureau, Government of India, Ministry of Road Transport & Highways, 03-January-2019 17:03 IST Ref: India-Myanmar-Thailand Trilateral Highway. https://mea.gov.in/press release).
22. *James* C. *Scott. 2009.* 'The Art of Not Being Governed'. Yale University Press ISBN 9780300152289
23. (https://mea.gov.in/lok-sabha.htm?dtl/31574/QUESTION_NO2840_INFRASTRUCTURE_DEVELOPMENT_IN_BHUTAN_AND_BANGLADESHLOK SABHA Question)
24. *Ibid.*
25. *Ibid.*

Thus MEA stepping induring this period of pandemic to carry out the structured and co-ordinate response with other ministries and other countries is commendable. It had never done at this scale and urgency before and it stood up to this challenge commendably. All this has helped India emerged as a leader in this region, on whom its partners trust and believe they can count on. This set the background for subsequent actions India could take during the Russia-Ukraine conflict.

Notes

1. 'COVID-19 Pandemic', Wikipedia https://covid19.who.int/WHO coronavirus COVID-19 Dashboard, as of Globally, as of 6:19pm CET, (referred to on13 February 2023 by author).
2. 'Pandemic', Wikipedia https://en.wikipedia.org/wiki/Pandemic (referred to on 5/1/2023 by author)
3. *Op. cit.*
4. Gebru, Addis Adera *et al.* 'Global Burden of COVID-19: Situational Analyis and Review'. 1 Jan. 2020: 1 – 10 WHO—Research article. https://covid19.who.int/table dashboard.
5. 'Question answer hub.' WWW.WHO.int/Question and Answer hub/ Coronavirus disease (COVID-19): Vaccines/Q&A/17 May 2022.
6. MEA Annual Report (2020-2021) (https://www.mea.gov.in/Uploads/ PublicationDocs/33569_MEA_annual_Report.pdf
7. *Ibid.*
8. MEA Annual Report (2021-2022) (https://www.mea.gov.in/Uploads/ PublicationDocs/33569_MEA_annual_Report.pdf
9. Guidelines for international arrivals 2020 https://www.mea.gov.in/ guidelines-for-international-arrivals.htm
10. LOK SABHA STARRED QUESTION NO.190 TO BE ANSWERED ON 10.12.2021 EMIGRANTS JOB LOSS DUE TO COVID-19, https://www.mea.gov.in/lok-sabha.htm?dtl/34630/question+no190+emigrants+job+loss+due+to+covid19)
11. *Op. cit.*
12. *Op. cit.*
13. Mutual recognition of COVID-19 Vaccination certificate, Dec.2021 (https://www.mea.gov.in/Mutual-recognition-Covid-vaccination-certificates.htm
14. Vaccine Maitri, Jan 2021 https://www.mea.gov.in/vaccine-maitri.htm

5

Russia-Ukraine Conflict

Emergence of India as a Global Leader

Introduction

India's foreign policy has four clearly-stated principles that have been practised over the past seven years, namely taking care of national trade and security interests (including using aggressive defence if needed), helping its citizens in foreign countries, taking care of partner countries, and continuing to participate in global governance organizations and institutions while maintaining its non-aligned stand. India over the last seven years has initiated various foreign policy strategies: Act East Policy, *Sagar* (trans-ocean) Outlook, Gulf Engagement and Central Asia strategies that have focused on resource use, humanitarian aid, and defence. Greater investment in defence strategies can be done through strengthening national defence, providing maritime security with India's neighbours in the Indian Ocean and Arabian Sea, and restructuring the defence organization. As a first responder, India takes on a leadership role for its partner countries that are in need of disaster management. Over the last few years, India has taken on the leadership of the global south and engaged with the United Nations as a temporary member.

India's foreign policy strategy has been to engage in diplomacy while finding solutions to issues. India continues to engage with

Revolution	Indicator	Immediate	Long-term Impacts
	Inequality	Weak companies, small businesses, and lowest wage earners disproportionately affected	First increase in global poverty since 1998; bigcompanies get bigger
	Labor Dislocation	Largest simultaneous job losses globally in nearly a century	Uneven recovery affecting most vulnerable workers, companies, and industries; increased obstacles to new business formation
	Innovation	Jump in online commerce, surge in digital payments	Digital wallets and shadow banks proliferate; online currencies gain value and a greater share of global transactions

Security

Revolution	Indicator	Immediate	Long-term Impacts
Security	Expanding National Security	Health security elevated as core national security	Growing debt pressures reduce defense spending
	Fragmentation	U.S. and Chinese leadership failures deepen global fragmentation	Future organizing principles for the Interbational system unclear
	Gray Zone	Countries intensify gray zone actions as they avoid conventional conflict and seek advantages	Low defense budgets and increased fragmentation drive even more gray zone activities
	Return to Terror	Increased activity by violence extremist organization (VEOs)	VEOs prey on weakened states, economic vulnerability to push ideology and influence

Governance

Revolution	Indicator	Immediate	Long-term Impacts
Governance	Political Awakening	Surging citizen expectations for change; mass protests (core triggers: inequality and injustice)	Friction between public expectations and governement responsiveness leads to long-term unrest or structural reform
	Democratic Decline	Crisis-driven authoritarian consolidation	Continued struggle between forces of democracy and authoritarianism
		Failed responses by populist leaders and governments	
	Trust	Surge in initial trust in government and expertise	Enduring trust deficit among youngest adult generations (especially Millennials)

Source: https://www.csis.org/analysis/covid-19-reshapes-future.

Notes

1. Minister of External Affairs. June 7, 2022. '8 Years of Modi Government: Transforming External Engagements' (gathering of the diplomatic corps in New Delhi). "https://www.mea.gov.in/Speeches-Statements.htm?dtl/35396/Address_by_External_Affairs_Minister_Dr_S_Jaishankar_at_the_event__8_Years_of_Modi_Government_Transforming_External_Engagements
2. Menon, S. May 2020. 'India's Foreign Affairs Strategy'. IMPACT SERIES by Distinguished Fellow. Brookings India. https://www.brookings.edu/wp-content/uploads/2020/05/India27s-foreign-affairs-strategy.pdf
3. Bapat, J. November, 2020 'Parameters for Developing Cross Boarder Sustainable Infrastructure', Paper 56, Gateway House, Mumbai
4. *Op. cit.*
5. Brannen, Samuel. Ahmed, Habiba. and Newton, Henry. 2020. 'COVID-19 Reshapes the Future' Centre for Strategic and International Studies (CSIS) (2020) Stable URL: https://www.jstor.org/stable/resrep25198

per cent prescribed for priority sector lending, they could not achieve the target of 18 per cent prescribed for finance to agriculture.

Shortfall in lending to priority sector/agriculture is allocated for contribution to the Rural Infrastructure Development Fund (RIDF) established with NABARD for assisting State Governments/State-owned corporations in quick completion of on-going projects relating to medium and minor irrigation, soil conservation, watershed management and other forms of rural infrastructure. In the case of RIDF-I to VI, the rate of interest on deposits placed on the Fund was uniform for all the banks irrespective of the extent of their shortfall. Effective RIDF VII, the rate of interest on RIDF deposits is linked to the banks' performance in lending to agriculture. Accordingly, banks receive interest at rates inversely proportional to their shortfall in agricultural lending. In other words, banks having higher shortfall will get lower rate of interest.

It may be observed from the above that banks have to make special efforts to increase flow of credit to agriculture. The main role of credit in agriculture is to transform conventional farming to modern farming for improving production and income level of farmers. Credit is required for adopting new technology and buying necessary inputs for the same. Credit is also required to take up subsidiary occupation in activities allied to agriculture for increasing income and reducing unemployment, rural poverty and rural-urban migration.

Coverage of the Book

Inclusion of an activity in lending to agriculture ensures increasing flow of credit by banks to it. Details of various activities included in 'direct' and 'indirect' finance to agriculture are given in the next chapter. In order to have a uniform approach, Reserve Bank of India issues guidelines from time to time regarding various aspects of lending to agriculture and other segments of priority sector. Present position of common guidelines are given in a separate chapter.

As Kisan Credit Cards have become very popular in place of crop loans to meet requirement of production credit,

2 Activities included in Agriculture

Finance provided by banks to agriculture is divided into two parts, viz., direct and indirect. A list has been circulated by the Reserve Bank to indicate the activities included in direct and indirect finance to agriculture. A few changes have been made from time to time in the activities included in the agricultural finance. Present position is as under:-

Direct finance to agriculture includes short, medium and long term loans given for agriculture and allied activites (dairy, fishery, piggery, poultry, bee-keeping, etc.) directly to individual farmers, Self Help Groups (SHGs) or Joint Liablity Groups (SLGs) of individual farmers without limit and to others (such as corporates, partnership firms and institutions) up to certain limits for taking up agriculture/ allied activities. Details of activities included in direct and indirect finance to agriculture have been circulated by the Rerserve Bank in its circular RDCD NO. Plan B.C. 84/04.09.01/ 2006-07 dated April 30, 2007. A copy of the same is given in the Annexure to this chapter.

Targets for Direct/Indirect Agricultural Lending

As ultimate objective of agricultural credit whether 'direct' or 'indirect' is to help the agricultural production,

(viii) The benefits under the scheme are as under:

(a)	Death due to accident (within 12 months of the accident) caused by outward, violent and visible means	Rs.50,000/-
(b)	Permanent total disability	Rs.50,000/-
(c)	Loss of two limbs or two eyes or one limb and one eye	Rs.50,000/-
(d)	Loss of one limb or one eye	Rs.25,000/-

(ix) The banks may ensure to incorporate the name of the Nominee in the Kisan Credit Card-cum-Pass Book.

(x) A simplified claim settlement procedure has been evolved under the Scheme whereby an Enquiry-cum-Verification Committee comprising representatives of the Branch Manager of the implementing bank, Lead Bank Officer and the insurance company would certify the nature of the accident causing disability/death and recommend settlement of insurance claims.

11. Clarifications on operational issues regarding insurance scheme

Clarifications on certain operational issues raised during the implementation of the insurance scheme are as under:

Sl.No.	Issues	Clarification
(i)	Is it possible to assign the policy in the name of the financing bank to enable it to recover outstanding dues in case of deceased KCC holders?	Unlike life policies, general insurance policies (except marine insurance) cannot be assigned. However, insurance companies are routing the claim amount through banks.
(ii)	Is it possible to nominate the policy in favour of the bank and adjust the claim amount to liquidate	This can be done provided KCC holder agrees to do so. But it is pertinent to note that nomination gives the right to receive the payment and not

Sl.No.	Issues	Clarification
	the liability of the farmer with the bank?	for appropriation of the same. Hence, it may be necessary to have the right of appropriation of the claim amount.
(iii)	Can KCC holders whose account are irregular be covered under the scheme?	All the KCC holders can be covered against the risk of accidental death or disability. If banks can arrange for the payment of premia alongwith the name of the nominee of the borrower, insurance companies will provide risk cover under the scheme, even if the account is irregular.
(iv)	Insurance cover for joint KCC holders	Being a personal accident insurance cover, all joint account holders can be covered individually under the scheme. Premium at the rate of Rs.15/- per borrower per year has to be paid in respect of all joint KCC holders who are to be covered under the scheme. There would not be any concession in premium for joint accounts. If all the joint KCC holders are not individually covered, the cover will be restricted to the first named KCC holder in the books or the person named specifically by the bank while remitting the premium.
(v)	Restriction of age : 70 years	As per the Insurance Act, maximum age for cover is fixed at 70 years for any class of insurance. Hence, this cannot be waived. Age ceiling is reckoned with reference to

available in the area. Spacing between the existing wells and proposed wells should also be according to the recommendations made in the geological survey for the area.

(ii) It should be ensured that the applicant has adequate area of land for full utilization of the irrigation resources likely to be created with the construction of the proposed well. If not, demand from neighbouring farmers for purchasing water may be assessed.

(iii) If the pumpset is to be operated by a diesel engine, it may be ensured that the diesel oil engine of the appropriate horse-power is readily available in the market. It may also be ensured that sufficient diesel oil is available in the area.

(iv) If the pumpset is to be operated by electricity, it may be ensured that electric supply will be made available uninterruptedly at the appropriate time. If electric supply is not certain, provision may be made for stand-by diesel engine depending on the size of the farm and its availability.

(v) The horse-power of the engine and size of the pumpset should be appropriate for the depth of the well and quantity of water to be lifted from the well.

(vi) The proposed engine should be of the standard make with ISI mark and be in common use in the area. If the applicant desires to go for an unusual make, an enquiry may be made to know the reasons for preferring an unusual make and also the arrangements made by the manufacturing firm for after sales service.

(vii) It may be ascertained that the necessary spare parts and after-sales service will be available in the area.

(viii) In case of lift irrigation from rivers, it should be ensured that the permission of the concerned authorities (Collector/Irrigation Department) is obtained.

(ix) The area proposed to be irrigated should be leveled and field channels provided so that water could be easily distributed. Hence, if any land development is necessary, the cost of such development should also be included in the cost of the proposal.

(x) If it is necessary to construct a shed for the protection of the engine or pumpset, provision should be made in the proposal for the cost of construction of the same.

(xi) In case of drip irrigation, water is applied at low pressure over a long period of time at frequent intervals directly into the plants' root zone through network of main lines, sub-mains and lateral lines. In addition to ensuring availability of water, item-wise breakup of unit cost should be ascertained.

(xii) In case of proposals relating to installation of sprinkler irrigation system, following points may be studied to ensure that the proposed sprinkler irrigation system will be successfully installed and maintained.

(a) Availability of water - source, quality and adequacy

(b) Area to be irrigated per sprinkler set

(c) Topography of land, e.g., contours, average slope, etc.

(d) Average wind speed (kmph.) and climate of scheme area

(e) Crops proposed to be grown/irrigated

(f) Frequency of irrigation and gross water requirement per irrigation

(g) Source of power

(h) Layout of sprinkler lines

(i) Type of sprinkler nozzles and spray diameter

(j) Calculation of pressure head required to be developed for the selected nozzles.

(k) Length and diameter of main line

1	2	3	4
8	Mangoes	Uttar Pradesh 27th Nov 2001	Saharanpur, Muzzafarnagar, Bijnaur, Meerut
9	Grapes and Grape Wine	Maharashtra 27th Nov 2001	Nasik, Sangli, Pune, Satara, Ahmednagar and Sholapur
10	Mango Pulp & Fresh Vegetables	Andhra Pradesh 23rd Jan 2002	Chittor District
11	Pineapple	Tripura 23rd Jan 2002	Kumarghat, Manu, Melaghar, Matabari and Kakraban Blocks
12	Potatoes, Onion and Garlic	Madhya Pradesh 23rd Jan	Malwa, Ujjain, Indore, Dewas, Dhar, Shajapur, Ratlam, Nimach and Mandsaur
13	Mango	Maharashtra 23rd Jan 2002	Districts of Ratnagiri, Sindhudurg, Raigarh and Thane
14	Apples	Jammu & Kashmir 23rd Jan 2002	Districts of Srinagar, Baramula, Anantnag, Kupwara, Badgaum and Pulwama
15.	Flowers	Tamil Nadu 27th Nov 2001	Dharmapuri
16	Lychee	West Bengal 27th Nov 2001	Districts of Murshidabad, Malda, 24 Pargana (N) and 24 Pargana (S)

1	2	3	4
17	Lychee	Bihar 5th Mar 2002	Muzaffarpur, Samastipur, Hajipur, Vaishali, East and West Champaran, Bhagalpur, Begusarai, Khagaria, Sitamarhi, Sarannd Gopalqani
18	Kesar Mango	Maharashtra 5th Mar 2002	Districts of Aurangabad, Jalna, Beed, Latur, Ahmednagar and Nasik
19	Walnut	Jammu & Kashmir 5th Mar 2002	Kashmir Region - Baramulla, Anantnag, Pulwama, Budgam, Kupwara and Srinagar / Jammu Region - Doda, Poonch, Udhampur, Rajouri and Kathua
20	Flowers	Uttranchal 23rd Apr 2002	Districts of Dehradun, Pantnagar
21	Mango & Vegetables	Gujarat 23rd Apr 2002	Districts of Ahmedabad, Khaida, Anand, Vadodra, Surat, Navsari, Valsad, Bharuch and Narmada
22	Flowers	Maharashtra 5th Mar 2002	Pune, Nasik, Kolhapur and Sangli
23	Potatoes	West Bengal 23rd Apr 2002	Districts of Hoogly, Burdwan, Midnapore (W) Uday Narayanpur and Howrah
24	Rose Onion	Karnataka 13th Jun 2002	Bangalore (Urban), Bangalore (Rural), Kolar

1. Production Process/Technology

If production can be achieved by using alternative raw materials with alternate process routes, a comparative study should be done to choose the most suitable process. It is easier to follow a conventional process. However, it should be ascertained whether any developments are taking place that might make the conventional process obsolete in the foreseeable future. If a new process is developed which is more economical, it should be preferred for setting up new units provided it is suitable to our country. A process from a foreign country should not be adopted blindly without giving due consideration to local conditions. Similarly, necessary study should be done to ensure that a process developed in a research laboratory will be successful on a commercial scale.

2. Arrangements for Technical Know-how

It may be ensured that satisfactory arrangements have been made to obtain necessary technological know-how required for the proposed production process. The technical know-how can be procured from the following sources:-

(i) Foreign Collaborators

(ii) Consultancy Organisations

(iii) Machinery Suppliers

(iv) Promoter's knowledge and experience

(v) Recruitment of suitable technical personnel

If promoters have entered into an agreement with foreign collaborators, the terms and conditions of the agreement may be studied.

If it is proposed to obtain assistance from consultancy organisations (local and/or foreign) for setting up the project, the experience of such organisations should be ascertained to ensure that they will be able to execute such assignments. The extent to which such organisations will provide necessary assistance may be ascertained and it may be ensured that promoters have necessary expertise with them to carry out the remaining work. The fees payable to such consultancy organisations should also be reasonable.

If it is proposed to enter into a turnkey contract with the machinery suppliers, it may be ensured that all aspects of project execution and initial operations (including performance guarantee) are covered in the contract.

If no collaborator/consultancy organisation/machinery supplier on turnkey basis is involved, it may be ensured that either promoters are competent enough to supervise the implementation of the project or they appoint competent technical experts for it. They should also recruit at the appropriate time suitable technical staff to implement the project and continue the production.

3. Size of the Project

Size of the project depends on the production process, availability of raw material/inputs, capital investment needed and the size of the market. Generally, a large size unit is more economical than a small size unit, but if the establishment of a large size unit needs heavy capital investment or the demand in the market is not sufficient for production at such level or sufficient inputs are not available for large size unit, it may be better to setup a plant of small size.

4. Product-mix/Product range

Product-mix may be decided according to market requirements. Production of certain items may have to be done in different sizes and quality to suit different consumers. If possible, the plant may have flexibility to change product-mix according to change in the market conditions. If such a flexibility needs additional investment, its impact on the viability of the project may be studied.

5. Selection of Plant and Machinery

Selection of plant and machinery should be done according to manufacturing process and size of the unit. Different stages of manufacturing process should have proper balance of capacity. For example, a product has to pass through 4 stages and the capacity of proposed machinery for each stage is as follows:

Production Cycle

	Stages	I	II	III	IV	
Raw material	Capacity	90	80	60	80	Finished Goods

the financial institutions may have to make unnecessarily higher commitments and promoters may divert resources for other purposes. It is needless to state that estimation of capital cost of the project is necessary not only in the interest of entrepreneurs but also in the interest of banks. Therefore, following guidelines have been prepared to give an idea to the entrepreneurs about the estimation of the capital cost and to the banks for appraisal of the estimates given by the entrepreneurs:

Details of Capital Cost of the Project and Methods of Appraisal

	Items to be included	Documents/Particulars to be scrutinized for appraisal
A. Land and Site Developments	I. Cost of Land II. Legal charges for Registration III. Cost of levelling IV. Cost of laying roads V. Cost of fencing VI. Cost of gates	I. Ascertain that land is sufficient for the project and possible further expansion II. Agreement for purchase of land III. Rates of legal charges and registration fee IV. Total area of roads and cost per square metre V. Total area of fencing and the basis on which provision has been made.
B. Buildings	I. Factory buildings II. Administrative buildings III. Godowns IV. Canteen, Guest houses, etc.	I. Design of buildings II. Different types of construction and area under each type of construction III. Ascertain from plant layout whether pro-

	V. Quarters for essential staff VI. Tanks, wells, etc. VII. Cost of sewers, drainages, etc. VIII. Architect's fee	posed construction of buildings is sufficient and also no unnecessary construction is done IV. Rate per square metre of each construction V. Agreement with Building Contractor, if any VI. A note on past record of Building Contractor and Architect
C. Plants & Machinery	(a) **IMPORTED PLANTS** I. F.O.B. value of plant to be imported II. Shipping, freight and insurance charges III. Import duty IV. Clearing, loading, unloading and transportation charges	I. Ensure that proposed import of plant is necessary II. Ensure that necessary stores and spares are also imported III. Quotations of plant to be imported IV. Orders, if already placed of plant to be imported V. Import licence, if required VI. Report of an independent engineer, if second-hand plant is being imported.
	(b) **INDIGENOUS PLANTS** I. Main plant and other machineries II. Machinery stores and spares	I. List of main items of machinery to be purchased-Ensure that all items are included and they have proper balance of capacity II. Quotations received from various mac-

(vii) Depreciation to total cost

(viii) Other residuary cost to total cost.

We shall now discuss various components of each ratio and also utility of each ratio to study the financial position and working of a unit.

1. Debt-Equity Ratio (Term Liabilities to Owned Funds)

This ratio indicates the relationship between term liabilities and owned funds and helps in assessing the capital gearing. A certain amount of equity is necessary to have cushion for debt. Higher the debt equity ratio, lower will be the margin available to the banker for its term loans.

All items of capital and liabilities can be divided into (a) current liability, (b) long term liability and (c) equity on the basis of the period during which the liability is repayable. The installments of the term debt repayable within one year and preference capital redeemable within one year should be treated as current liability and excluded for the purpose of long term debt-equity ratio. Similarly, fixed deposits repayable after one year should be treated as long term debt for the purpose of long term debt-equity ratio and excluded from current liabilities. Preference share capital, sales tax loan and other incentive loans should be treated as quasi-equity and they may be included in equity only upto the period of time when their redemption/repayment is due after three years. Thereafter, the preference shares/sales-tax or other incentive loans should be treated as part of liabilities.

The following items should be included in debt:

(i) Long term loans/deposits

(ii) Debentures - convertible debentures to be treated as debt (except that part of debentures which is compulsorily convertible into equity) until they are converted.

(iii) Preference share capital redeemable within three years

(iv) Sales tax loan repayable within three years

(v) Other incentive loans repayable within three years

(vi) Future lease rentals payable

(vii) Working capital term loan
(viii) External commercial borrowings
(ix) Foreign suppliers' credit
(x) Deferred credit
(xi) Deferred interest
(xii) Unsecured loans and deposits

It may be noted that the installments of all the above dues payable within one year should be deducted from the total to arrive at the figure of long term debt because any liability is considered as long term debt when it is repayable after one year and as current liability when it is repayable within one year.

The following items should be included in the equity:-

(i) Equity share capital
(ii) Preference share capital redeemable after three years
(iii) Any other types of share capital
(iv) Free reserves and surplus. However, reserves created out of revaluation of assets are excluded
(v) Subsidy
(vi) Sales-tax loan repayable after three years
(vii) Other incentive loans repayable after three years
(viii) Subordinated loans from promoters not repayable without the permission of financing bank
(ix) Portion of debentures to be compulsorily converted into equity shares

Accumulated losses, arrears of depreciation, preliminary expenses to the extent not written off and goodwill should be deducted from the above total to arrive at the figure of equity.

The debt-equity ratio is normally allowed around 1.5:1 depending on the nature of the project, size of the project, priority of the project, gestation period involved, profitability potential, debt-service, capacity of the project, risk involved in the project, etc. Higher debt-equity ratio can be allowed for large size capital intensive units. Similarly, a liberal debt-equity ratio is allowed in respect of projects set up in under

As profitability index of project X is more than that of project Y, it can be concluded that project X is better than project Y. Higher the profitability index better is the project.

Internal Rate of Return

Net present value method indicates the net present value of the cash flows of a project at the pre-determined interest rate, but it does not indicate the rate of return of the project. In order to find out the rate of return of a project, estimated net cash flows of each year are discounted at various rates till a rate is obtained at which the sum of positive present values is equal to the sum of negative present values or the net present value comes to zero. Such a rate is called internal rate of return. In other words, internal rate of return is that rate of discount which would equate the present value of investments (cash outflows) to the present value of benefits (cash inflows) over the life of the project.

Internal rate of return cannot be determined by just looking at the cash flows. It is calculated by trial and error method. Various discounting rates are applied to the net cash flows until a rate is found that reduces the net present value to zero. Usually cut-off rate is chosen at the starting point. If net present value at the cut-off rate comes positive, the internal rate of return is further calculated by increasing the discounting rate. If net surplus comes negative, the discounting rate is reduced. The exercise is done till a rate is found when the present value of net cash flow comes to zero. As this is a tedious and time consuming process, an interpolation formula can be used after arriving at a range between which the internal rate of return lies. The example of project 'A' given earlier while explaining net present value method can be used to demonstrate the calculation of internal rate of return. First the cash flows are discounted as 15% as already done in the illustration of net present value method. As net surplus comes positive at 15 per cent, the cash flows are discounted at 20 per cent. As net surplus comes positive even at 20 per cent, the cash flows are discounted at 25 percent as follows :-

(Amount in Rs.)

Cash flow	Discounting factor at 15%	Present value at 15% (1×2)	Discounting factor at 20%	Present value at 20% (1×2)	Discounting factor at 25%	Present value at 25% (1×2)
(1)	(2)	(3)	(4)	(5)	(6)	(7)
Year 0 -1000	-	1000.0	-	1000.0	-	1000.0
Year 1 +300	0.870	+261.0	0.833	+249.9	0.800	+240.0
Year 2 +400	0.756	+302.4	0.694	+277.6	0.640	+256.0
Year 3 +400	0.658	+263.2	0.579	+231.6	0.512	+204.8
Year 4 +300	0.572	+171.6	0.482	+144.6	0.410	+123.0
Year 5 +300	0.497	+149.1	0.402	+120.6	0.328	+98.4
Net Present Value		=147.3		=24.3		-77.8

As the net present value comes positive at 20 per cent and negative at 25 per cent, the internal rate of return should be between 20% and 25%.

In order to arrive at internal rate of return, the following interpolation formula can be used:-

Interpolation formula

Internal rate of return =

Lower discount rate+Difference between the two

$$\text{discount rates} \times \left(\frac{\text{Net Present Value at the lower Discount Rate}}{\text{Absolute difference between the net present value at the two discounting rates}} \right)$$

$$= 20 + 5 \times \frac{24.3}{24.3 + 77.8}$$

$$= 20 + 5 \times \frac{24.3}{102.1}$$

= 20+1.19 = 21.19 or Say 21%.

(iv) Residential as well as business addresses of the borrowers and guarantors should be furnished while making the application to the Tribunal so that time is not wasted in serving the summons on the defendants.

(v) The bank should also submit balance confirmation duly signed by the borrower about the outstanding amount or a statement of account acknowledged by the borrower or acknowledged balance sheet.

(vi) If mortgage is available to the bank, the application made under Section 19 of the Recovery Act should also include a further application for interim order seeking attachment of mortgaged property.

(vii) Operational departments should not develop the tendency of forgetting the loan account as soon as papers are transferred to Law/Recovery Department. If he Law/Recovery Department should be given consistent backing by operational departments till the recovery certificate stands executed.

(viii) A Quarterly review should be prepared and placed before the Executive Committee/Management Committee of the bank giving the position of the cases filed before the Tribunals. Proper follow-up of the applications filed before the Tribunal is necessary to avoid delay.

It may be observed from the above that banks should take advantage of the Tribunals by taking necessary steps without wasting time. It is hoped that establishment of Debt Recovery Tribunals may induce borrowers to enter into settlements with banks.

8. Change in repayment period

Borrowers may not be able to repay according to the repayment schedule due to any of the following reasons:-

(i) Shorter repayment period

(ii) Shorter grace period

(iii) Incomplete investments

(iv) Infructuous investments

(v) Natural calamities

(vi) Relief to farmers affected by natural calamities for atleast two successive years

(vii) Relief to farmers in distress due to factors other than natural calamities

It may be necessary for the banks to rephase the repayment of loans and take corrective steps in the above circumstances. While rephasing the loans, banks may have to take care to adhere to the necessary legal formalities required in respect of documentation. Banks may undertake case by case study of overdues to ascertain whether the borrower is not able to repay the loan due to anyone of the above reasons and whether it is necessary to rephase the repayment schedule as follows:

(I) Shorter repayment period

Banks should fix repayment schedule on the basis of the expected incremental income likely to accrue to the borrower. On the basis of scientific study of the economics of various schemes of agriculture, NABARD has suggested repayment schedules for various purposes. Repayment period schedule suggested by NABARD for term loans provided to small farmers is given at the end of this chapter as Annexure. If the banks have fixed shorter repayment period, they may re-examine such cases and rephase their repayment schedule. Banks should first work out the amount of repayment instalments on the basis of full permissible repayment period of the loan and taking the basis, allow the number of years in which the loan outstanding together with interest could be repaid. For example, a bank has given a loan of Rs. 15,000/- for a purpose for which permissible period of repayment is 15 years. However, it has fixed repayment period for 9 years only. If Rs. 3000/- is currently outstanding, the repayment period may be extended by three year and not six years because on the basis of 15 years period,

(1)	(2)	(3)	(4)	(5)
16.	Buffaloes	4-5	Monthly/ Quarterly	-do-
17.	Graded Murrah Buffaloes	4-5	Monthly/ Quarterly	-do-
18.	Cross-bred Calf Rearing	5-6	Monthly/ Quarterly	30 months
19.	Sheep Breeding	5	Half Yearly	12 months
20.	Piggery	4-5	Yearly	12 months
21.	Goat rearing	4-5	Quarterly /Half Yearly /Yearly	12 months
22.	Poultry	6-7	Half Yearly	12 months
23.	Duckery	4-5	Quarterly/ Half Yearly	12 months
24.	Camel	5	Half Yearly/ Yearly	-
25.	Camel and Cart	5-7	Quarterly/ Half Yearly	-
26.	Bullocks	4	Half Yearly/ Yearly	-
27.	Bullocks and Cart	5-7	Quarterly/ Half Yearly	-
28.	Animal drawn Carts	5-7	Quarterly/ Half Yearly	-

(1)	(2)	(3)	(4)	(5)
29.	Jhota Buggi	4	Quarterly/ Half Yearly	-
30.	Marine Fisheries a. Non-mechanised boat	4-7	Monthly (excluding monsoon period)	No instalments in 4 months each year
	b. Mechanised boat	8-12	-do-	-do-
31.	Inland Fisheries a. Pond Fish Culture	5-8	Half Yearly	11 months
	b. Brackish water fish/Prawn culture	5-10	Half Yearly	11 months
32.	Sericulture a. New Plantation	4	Half Yearly	11 months
	b. Equipment	3		
	c. Rearing House	5		
	d. Cottage Basin	7		
	e. Wiremesh	3		
	Plantation Horticulture			
33.	Cashew Plantation	12-15	Yearly	6-7 Years
34	Mango Plantation	12-15	Yearly	6-7 Year
35.	Lime/Citrus Plantation	10-15	Yearly	5 Years
36.	Guava Plantation	10-15	Yearly	4-5 Years
37.	Sapota Plantation	10-15	Yearly	5-6 Years
38.	Ber Plantation	10-15	Yearly	4-5 Years
39.	Acid Lime Plantation	10-15	Yearly	4-5 Years

find me a place from which I can get a commanding view of the battle-field. I shall be there at six." Then he throws himself on the camp-bed, and instantly falls asleep.

In the course of that night, a Prussian headquarters staff is informed by its scouts that remarkable movements are going on among the French troops. Oh, well, tomorrow will be time enough to discuss the matter! But before the day dawns, the Emperor has ridden along the front, has fired his guard with enthusiasm, has recalled the day of Austerlitz.

He defeats the Prussians near Jena, while simultaneously Davoust is routing a superior force of the enemy at Auerstädt.

When the valiant Duke of Brunswick is fatally wounded, no one ventures to take over the command. They all lose their heads, and what is left of the army of the great Frederick flees in disorder through Saxony eastward.

"Chère amie, I did some fine manœuvring against the Prussians, and won a great victory yesterday. Twenty thousand prisoners, and we took about a hundred cannon and colours.... Have been camping here for a couple of days. I'm feeling splendid. Farewell. Take good care of yourself, and love me."

In Weimar, he meets the reigning duchess. Charles Augustus, the Duke, has been in a warlike frame of mind for the last twenty years. He is Prussophil, and, in defiance of advice, has joined issue with the Emperor. Now, as Prussian general, he is in full flight after the disaster at Jena. No one knows his whereabouts. The court has also fled from Weimar. Only the duchess and her minister, Goethe, remain behind. When the Emperor sees the lady for the first time, he says: "I am sorry for you! How could the Duke ...!" But to his amazement (for he is always against women's rule—in especial, when the woman happens to be a German) the duchess answers him with so much clarity, simplicity, and dignity, explains the duke's friendship with Prussia in so steadfast a manner, that he is shaken, behaves courteously, returns in the evening in order to have to long talk with her, and, after having vowed the annihilation of her dynasty, promises her that nothing shall be done to injure the duchy. Why?

criticism in these pretty phrases. But he adds: "A handsome young man, more intelligent than is usually supposed." At a later date, Napoleon utters profound truths regarding Alexander: "The tsar is an attractive figure, well formed to exercise a victorious charm on those with whom he comes in contact. Had I been inclined to surrender to superficial impressions, I should have become devoted to him instantly. But there is something peculiar about him, which I can best express by saying that in all he is and does there seems to be somethings lacking. The strangest point about the matter is that it is impossible to foresee precisely what will be lacking in any given instance, for the defect is infinitely variable." Thus, the man whose friendship is all-important to him seems to him utterly feminine. His final judgment takes the form of an overwhelming compliment: "Were Alexander a woman, I think I should fall passionately in love with him."

It is not surprising that such a man should in a trice be mastered by the seductions of the man of power; nor is it remarkable that subsequently the Tsar should forsake the Emperor, for the surrender and the abandonment are both feminine. No one has ever given a better description of Alexander than Metternich: "A mingling of masculine merits with feminine defects; favourite ideas, imperfectly thought out, initiate sudden impulses. As a result, sudden embarrassments, He gives his word too quickly, and then finds it very difficult to keep; not strong enough for ambition in the grand style, and not weak enough for mere vanity; the man of the world rather than ruler. There is a sort of periodicity in his enthusiasms and disenchantments, a periodicity of five-year terms during which an idea waxes and wanes. At the close of each cycle, a new one opens. To begin with, he is a liberal. Then he is filled with hatred for the Frenchman; then he passes under the Frenchman's influence."

Five years hence, a new period will come to an end, and the friends of today will be at war gain.

Maybe Napoleon already foresees this in the splendid tent, where for two hours the emperors discuss the affairs of the world; certainly he foresees it during the long dinners and during the rides

The mother's heart stops beating for a moment. How she has enjoyed the last six months; the period of quiet intercourse with her son. An end to the tranquillity and the security! But Letizia is a proud woman and a clever one. She knows that nobody can hold him back when he has made up his mind, and that the only effect of anxious dissuasion will be to disturb his composure. She says:

"Follow your destiny. It cannot be God's will that you are to die from poison, or after an inactive old age; though it may well be his will that you are to die sword in hand. Let us put our trust in Mother Mary."

On the last evening, the authorities are summoned by their sovereign. He announces his imminent departure. "I have been extraordinarily well pleased here. As a sign of confidence, I am leaving my mother and my sister. To your care, too, I entrust this country, to which I attach great importance." The governor and the mayor express their lively regret. The tone befits the departure of a distinguished guest who has been spending a few months in a lovely island for the benefit of his health, and is sorry that the time has come for his return home.

He goes on board, and at dawn seven little frigates, carrying a thousand men and a few guns, set sail for the French coast. He stands on the deck. The outlines of Elba, where he has lived so peacefully, and of Corsica, where many years before he had made stormy attempts to force his way upwards, fade into the distance. Slowly the coast of the French Riviera begins to show clearly through the mists of the first day of March. Let us look into the Emperor's mind:

"What is the minimum? Defeat and death. What is the maximum? Europe? No use thinking any more about Europe! The dream of the United States of Europe is finished. I cannot get another million Frenchmen, and the foreign nations are not ready for my scheme. I must give France a constitution, and must accommodate myself to governing through Chambers. The time for dictatorships is over. Besides, we are not in Paris yet. What will the army do?"

But, as spiritual leader, the Emperor wins over his whilom enemy, Benjamin Constant, a friend of Madame de Stael. This old-time democrat, who had recently been thundering in the press against the brigand of Elba and comparing him to Attila and to Genghis Khan, is needed now that the Emperor proposes to govern through Chambers. Napoleon, therefore, invites Constant to an audience. The Emperor has not seen him for fifteen years. The interview, recorded by Constant, occupies four pages of print. We are shown, without periphrases, the last transformation of Napoleon, the statesman who was ever ready to adapt his course to the demands of practical politics.

"The nation again wishes for tribunes and assemblies. It has always wanted them, for it threw itself at my feet when I climbed to power.... I assumed less power than was actually conceded me. Today, all is otherwise. The preference for constitutions, for elections, for speeches, is again to the fore. This is, however, the desire of a minority. The majority desires myself, alone.... I am not only the soldiers' Emperor; I am also the Emperor of the workers and peasants.... Thus, in spite of all, the people comes back to me. I treat the people severely, I never flatter the people; and yet the people cries: 'Long live the Emperor!' This is because there are common bonds between us....

"It is otherwise with nobility. The nobles thronged my anterooms begging and receiving the posts they coveted.... But no common bond has ever existed between us. The horse submitted to the rider, it had been well trained; all the same, I felt it tremble beneath me.... Yes, I endeavoured to set up a world monarchy, and for this I needed unfettered power. Who, in my place, would not have wished to do likewise? Did not the world itself encourage me? Princes and subjects hastened to come beneath my sceptre's sway.... But if France is to be the whole of my dominos, then a constitution is better....

"Tell me your ideas. Freedom of speech, free elections, responsible ministers, freedom of the press? ... I am agreeable to all this. Especially the freedom of the press. To try and crush this any longer would be absurd.... I am the man of the people. If the